THE BOBBING BOATS

A Café in Borth-y-Gest

by

Mary Howe

Edited by Richard Walwyn

ISBN: 978-1-9163674-0-1

Published in 2020 by Delfryn Publications
Delfryn, Borth-y-Gest, Porthmadog, Gwynedd LL49 9TW
Telephone: +44(0)1766 512115
Website: www.delfrynpublications.co.uk

Cover designed by Cathy Woodhead from a sketch by Mary Howe

Contents

'The Grey Tea Room' by Meryl Watts

Editor's Introduction

Mary Howe, who was born in June 1909 and died in 1986, was the youngest of three sisters. The oldest, called Sarah but usually known as Sissie who was born in 1893, lived with Mary for most of her life. The middle sister was my mother, Fanny, born in 1903. There had been two other children who died in infancy. The three girls were brought up in Heywood in Lancashire where their father had a small printing and stationery business. Sarah, the oldest, took over the management of the family business when their father died in 1929, Fanny became a doctor and Mary – the artistic one – studied domestic science and horticulture at university, before eventually settling down at the age of thirty to run the Bobbing Boats café in Borth-y-Gest. The café belonged to Mary, but during the winter months Sarah and Mary moved first to a house in Prestbury and latterly to a flat in Harrogate, both belonging to Sarah. During the summer Sarah came to the café to help her sister run it, but particularly to look after the business affairs. My father who was a business man was frankly appalled by the seemingly casual way in which Mary managed the money. All transactions were done in cash held in an old-fashioned wooden till box kept in the cupboard under the stairs. He need not have worried for Sarah was more than capable of looking after it.

Both Sarah and Mary were quite eccentric in a benign way, and both had a very low opinion of men. Neither really came to terms with the fact that my mother had married – hard things were said – and my father found them both difficult, and Mary particularly infuriating. I was frankly scared of my Auntie Mary. I think my mother found her quite trying too, especially as she was a conventionally trained medic whilst Mary, apart from being devoted to homeopathy and the teachings of Rudolph Steiner was prone to poo-poo the ideas of people with whom she disagreed. She had strongly held opinions and disagreed quite a lot. Secretly we often knew that her vaunted 'science' was dodgy, but held our peace.

Mary typed this book during spare moments while running the café, and I have made very few editorial changes except to correct obvious typing errors. It is not obvious when it was written, but internal evidence points to the late 1960s. Much of it now seems very dated, but it is a product of its time and might be treated as a piece of social history. Mary had a number of what she would have called interests but are now described as 'passions'. She had strong views on design, cooking, art and music. She was highly sensitive to nuances of colour and was an accomplished water colourist. She was well-read in a very wide range of topics including Philosophy – she was an admirer of Bertrand Russell as well as Rudolph Steiner, and was a strong believer in reincarnation. She was well travelled. And, of course, she was a highly enthusiastic gardener and plants-woman. The tiny garden of the Bobbing Boats was remarkable and became her principal work of art.

The café was not to everyone's taste, particularly if what you were after was baked beans on toast or an ice cream – "if you want one of those go to Mrs Tibbs at the other end of the village." However she had a loyal following of regular customers who came back again and again. For many years after she had died and indeed even today, when the house is no longer a café, people often call in to say how much they had loved it, and it is for such people that this book has been published.

It is not Mary's only book. She also wrote a considerable tome on the Ladies of Llangollen, which was rejected by a publisher, not least because she entirely overlooked the emotional relationship between the Ladies, Eleanor Butler and Sarah Ponsonby. When a rival's book was published just after her effort was turned down she was not best pleased.

Those of us who knew the café in its heyday remember its minute kitchen from which issued a stream of teas – home-made soda bread, cakes, shortbread, biscuits and jam (always made from rhubarb, ginger, orange peel and sultanas and known as 'Glory Jam'). As children we used to call at the back door in the hope of being treated with 'gone wrongs' – overcooked and broken biscuits – but one had to summon up the nerve to do so as they were usually much too busy to tend to us.

As family we used to laugh quite a lot behind Mary's back. She was notoriously abstemious with food for herself and consequently was thin as a rake. As a child I was most impressed with her immensely long thin feet. On one memorable occasion she returned from a bracing walk along the beach path and announced that as she had had so much air she would not need to eat any more that day. When I first took my new wife to meet her, Jackie was surprised to be offered digestive biscuit sandwiches – that is a digestive biscuit between two slices of bread – because "digestives are a bit rich to eat on their own." I now think she may have been teasing.

The family still have much of the furniture Mary collected, together with her watercolours and pottery. The house is largely unchanged from its days as a café though sadly the garden is now a shadow of its former glory.

Richard Walwyn
Borth-y-Gest 2020

A postcard of Borth-y-Gest showing The Bobbing Boats

The house on its left was demolished to allow the building of the Tan y Foel road

Clematis – a painting by Mary Howe

Chapter I

The Beginnings

'Life is a bridge, pass over it but build no house thereon, for he that buildeth for a day buildeth for eternity'

I translated these words in lovely Arabic script from over the immense arched entrance to Akbar's Mosque in Fatehpur Sikri with the help of Baedeker. Their meaning I interpreted as I wished, missing their deeper implication. They mirrored what I then imagined to be my essential outlook on life. For me it was, I hoped, to be full of change, no settled job and no fixed abode.

How well we know ourselves! For over thirty years I did the same work in the same house and enjoyed it thoroughly.

I was twenty-seven at the time, on a visit to my sister Fanny in Bombay. Having a tiny income and the year being in the middle of the economic depression, I had made many excuses for not starting on any serious career after leaving the University with a pass degree in Science.

While I was in India I received a letter from my other and much older sister Sarah describing her visit to a café and craft shop in Anglesey. The friend who had taken her knew Ann, the pioneer who had started the business, and my sister thought running a café of this kind would be the very job for me. I replied that "I would not be found dead running a café."

When I returned to England the next May, Sarah engineered another visit to Anglesey. As soon as I saw the café I knew that this *was* the work I would best like to do.

Furnished with polished tables and oak chairs, and with hand-made pottery, wood ware and pictures displayed for sale around the low-ceilinged rooms, and with a garden where a sheltered arbour suggested outdoor meals with a superb view of the Snowdon mountains, it seemed to me quite perfect.

If I could find a place like this, preferably a long low cottage painted white I would be ready to start tomorrow. My house too should be in a village, no mere road house for me.

That summer we looked round the Lake District and the Cotswolds, but found nothing. Friends warned us not to add the Yorkshire Dales to our hunting ground because there the cooks were too good and one's standard would need to be very high to make a mark. They suggested rather that Wales was as good a place to look as any, because catering was not, at that time, particularly generous. A modest effort could well make one a fair reputation.

The following year Ann was threatened with an operation and, to enable her to rest and so hope to avoid the necessity of it, she asked me to go and help at her café for the summer. It was there that my ideas had a chance to crystallise, and I gained some idea of how to set about things. How I enjoyed that year! I did some of the baking, served in the café and helped to unpack the new stock. It was just the experience I needed.

The place was run with an adequate staff and a constant stream of amusing friends kept things lively. I noticed too that these visitors to the cottage were not the only friends, for customers came year after year and many of them had known Ann for years.

I realised that this was not due entirely to Ann's personality, so different in many ways from my own, but in no small part to geography. The café was in a village and a village, so to speak, at the end of a cul-de-sac, not merely on the way to somewhere else. People came to stay year after year. Or, if they merely came to look, there was a chance of their seeing the café twice, both on the inward and on the outward journey, and thereafter coming many times in the future.

It was a pity I had not been able to have this invaluable experience earlier because the year before when I was looking round I had burnt my fingers badly. Desperate to start, I arranged with a woman gardener whom I had worked for, that I would take a biggish house and sublet part of it to her so that she could make a business out of the garden.

I found a house which was too large and in an unsuitable place in Somerset. The friend realised the mistake in time and drew back but not before I had saddled myself with the property. The only thing to do was to sell quickly at considerable loss and start again. That loss was to influence my actions for many, many years for it meant that I had the barest minimum of capital to start with and every penny had to be counted. It did not however damp my enthusiasm and in many ways it helped by making me careful. It also made me appreciate any good fortune that came my way.

After this setback I determined to look for a small house similarly situated to Ann's. The village I was searching for introduced itself during the summer that I helped her, though I was not to find the house waiting for me just yet. My sister, on leave from India, was looking for a small seaside place where she could take her two young children. Friends told her of Borth-y-Gest. They had told me of it too, but I had never succeeded in getting there. However that summer I did so, as Ann suggested that before the season became really busy I should have a week with my little niece and nephew at Borth-y-Gest. I fell in love with the place immediately. While the children were being put to bed I used to sit on a seat at the point watching the soft lights playing over the hills opposite, and in the evening my sister and I would walk the hill paths and come back by the sea edge to sit once more and watch the wonderful summer sunset turning the sand momentarily to green, and the mountains first to pink, then cold grey and leaving the sky all the colours of a dove's wing. There were, of course, no houses for sale. It was there that I first met the mysterious word 'entail', for however dim the house, however old the occupants, we were told that there was no chance of an outsider getting hold of it because of a mysterious niece or nephew lurking somewhere, waiting for it to fall vacant.

The next spring I helped Ann again at Easter and later set off with my elder sister for another hunt. This time we stuck to Wales. We went to have another look at Borth-y-Gest and found a house on the front that had been sold a week before. It was to be pulled down. However, when I saw the number fourteen on the door, I felt sure that it was to have connections with me in some way. I have never been the sort of person who wins by guessing the correct weight of cakes, or the names of beautifully dressed dolls. The only thing I have ever drawn out of the hat of chance has been on three occasions a summons to the Jury. However at the age of nine I won a baby doll with a raffle ticket numbered fourteen. With some premonition of the arid future that luck of that kind was planning for me, I remembered that number.

The purchaser of Number 14 whom we should nowadays call a 'developer' was intending to build houses on the hillside behind and needed the space for an entry road. Rumbles of war were being heard however. Czechoslovakia had been 'liquidated' and it did not seem to be quite the time to be taking risks. These are taken more lightly in our present decade and things move quickly. The houses are planned once more, by another developer, the entry road has actually been made, but it has been the fate of the next door house, not of mine to make way for it.

So when, hardly daring to hope, we went in the spring of 1937 to ask if we could rent this Number 14 for the time being, the surprising answer came in the affirmative.

In case there should be restrictions on the property we told the agent-cum-solicitor the use to which the house was going to be put. He held out little hope of business opportunities. In fact he gave it as his private opinion that the village in which I was proposing to open my café was 'stagnant'. There seemed to be no objections on other grounds, however, so, on our signing to the effect that I would not sell fish and chips, burn bones, make glue, collect shoddy or carry on any noisome trade, an agreement for a yearly tenancy was drawn up.

The double-fronted Victorian villa of which I now found myself the tenant was mercifully the end one of a terrace of three so there was easy access up the side for deliveries. Behind it where we were told that some day houses would perch, stretched a narrow field, later in the year to have its contours outlined by rows of potatoes. Thickset oak woods hung over the sloping field and pleasant clumps of trees broke up the green sweep. In front our view was open to the estuary and the hills and mountains of Merioneth.

The heavy clumsy bay windows, one each side of the door to light the front parlour, struck me as ugly and ponderous and I planned to make them look even more conspicuous by painting them bright green. For had not the outside paint on the Anglesey café been green?

The left-hand parlour was very small, measuring only ten feet square, but behind it was a sizeable living kitchen reached by a narrow lobby alongside the steep brown-painted staircase. Here five brown doors met in conclave, the one leading from the hall attempting to shed some light on their deliberations through two panels of Muranese glass.

Opening the smallest of the five doors revealed the under-stairs; a region draped with cobwebs and smelling of whitewash and damp plaster which seemed to be perpetually dropping off, so would have to be imprisoned by tacking oilcloth from the floor to the wall supports. The new walls eventually painted white and the door removed we should have, I decided, a handy home for the till, standing on an emptied packing case.

How much remained to be done before the till could start to work, however, was revealed when I opened the remaining three doors. The largest one ahead with bolts and bars in triplicate led down a six-inch step into a 'back place', a later addition to the house whose floor was of slate and whose walls had been roughly plastered before receiving a coat or two of whitewash. From the 'back place' you gained the outside, an area of beaten ashes leading eventually to the tangle which even then I insisted on calling 'the garden'. I viewed the way down into the embryonic larder with considerable distaste, for being a rheumaticky family we have no love for unnecessary steps. But, to make use of an expression which has indeed worked hard over the years, I decided that for the 'TB' the step would have to stay. TB means 'time being' and when so many jobs and improvements are queuing up for a turn they have to spend a good deal of time in what governments euphemistically term 'the blue-print stage'.

The improvement had to be done eventually, the floor was raised and covered with red tiles and the undulating walls were boxed in with wood. The work was done just before wartime shortages made anything of the kind impossible, and at the same time the kitchen alterations, inevitable from the first, were also tackled.

Even with the addition that we made to it the kitchen is still small but it was even smaller then, being merely an oblong six foot by ten foot. The fourth door opened into it and revealed another flagged floor, walls painted a medium terracotta, and a shallow oblong slate sink without draining board of any kind let into the thickness of the wall below the window. Over the sink arched a solitary thin brass tap.

Apart from the shelves which mounted the walls almost up to the ceiling, the only other item of equipment was a large black gas oven which had even then already attained its legal majority.

The eyes of many gas board employees, calling to carry out repairs or perhaps to present questionnaires, used to light up in happy anticipation of a sale, when they espied my gas stove. But for years I obstinately refused to part with it for it was wonderfully even and easy to bake with. A modern one would look nicer and would be easier to keep clean but I am not sure whether I should actually find it any more reliable.

I decided that ivory oil-bound distemper should cover up the terracotta, but for the present I had to endure the flagged floor. Later, however, a thick layer of felt covered by linoleum tempered its hardness. Apart from a table bought for a few shillings at a saleroom the rest of the furniture was assembled from boxes and packing cases. At first these pieces had to be painted. Covered with plastic hardboard, some stayed long with me, for they were all light and easy to move and fitted the spaces beautifully. Other pieces made for specific needs were added later.

I grew so used to this equipment that I tended to forget its humble origins. It certainly administered rather a shock to a newly-demobbed ATS girl who asked if she could come and help me one spring. She arrived to find the larder filled with painted boxes and boards, for plastic surfaces were only just making their appearance. The kitchen was bare and in process of being decorated – gloss paint having some years ago superseded flaking distemper. The job finished, I asked her to bring in the furniture. "But where is it?" she asked, for she had imagined that the clutter in the larder was only awaiting a bonfire. She did not stay long for as she said she "could not settle down in Civvy Street." If all 'Civvy Street' was to prove as crazy as the Bobbing Boats, it was no wonder she was considering returning to the sanity of the ATS.

If the working kitchen was some years in reaching a state in which one could take any pride, the future of the living kitchen was very different. It was in fact quite soon to become the most pleasing room in the house. Its aspect helped in this because in the late afternoon, before setting behind the oak wood, the slanting sun shone through a pretty twelve-paned window. This window proved that I had maligned the house in calling it Victorian. And it may be remembered that thirty years ago we were not having second thoughts about architecture of that period, as we are doing today. The date of the houses was according to local tradition probably as early as 1840 and the front bay windows had been added much later[1]. The little terrace had been built to house the carpenters employed on the building of sailing ships. For these as for other things the district is a good deal better known than it was then.

Having admired the window I next felt the dividing wall and to my delight found that it was made of wood. With the help of a practical joiner we should be able next year to have a 'through room' with all that that would mean in extra light and a feeling of space.

A retired ship's carpenter was soon found and was immediately occupied in taking off the offending doors, fixing corner wardrobes and disguising furniture picked up at sales as well as more humble, but equally necessary jobs like making draining boards for the slate sink. I did not want to undertake big alterations until I saw how things worked out, especially as the house was not mine.

This living kitchen had obviously, for close on a hundred years, been the hub of the house. The wood floor was so worn that knots stood out on its surface - hard and shining. When I found myself sliding up and down on them I remembered from my early youth another floor like this. It had been in the day school in Lancashire in which the annual Church Sale of Work was held. Up and down those slippery knots the vicar's small son and I used to slither after tea, attempting to execute barn dances and polkas.

---

[1] The house was actually built in 1880, together with Ebenezer Chapel and the houses in between. Most houses at the time had small-paned sash windows at the back with larger paned windows on the front. The small panes could use thinner and therefore cheaper glass. Ed.

At the time of my first meeting with it, however, the living kitchen was far from being light and spacious in spite of its pretty window. On the outside wall was a diminutive black grate with which I mentally vowed to have no dealings whatever, for fires and I have never got on well together. To start with I am not clever at kindling them and when my back is turned they delight in taking a doze. Or I mistake it for a doze, only to find too late that it is indeed the sleep of death.

However, my sister is clever with fires and she recognised in this little black dwarf an economical way of heating water, for the house was supplied with cold taps only. So for a time a large copper kettle was to sit here dutifully on a small nest of fire and quietly keep us going.

My sister also kept us going in many other ways – the help I most welcomed being with the book-keeping. I once endured lessons in this art, but never cured myself of a tendency to put items on the wrong side of the page, thereby doubling the error. Mathematics was never my strong point though proportion sums in arithmetic always gave me pleasure and I really enjoyed Geometry. Euclid was all so beautifully reasonable. The rest of Greek culture, however, which we are supposed to absorb more or less through our pores, meant very little to me, except their architecture.

Buildings can exert an almost physical effect on me. When I saw the fifth century temple of Poseidon at Paestum recently I felt the joyous welcoming power, the loveableness of a Greek temple. The glorious weight and thrust as well as the happiness of this huge and simple building are all, I realise, the result of perfect proportion.

Proportion: perhaps this is the quality in life that most dodges, beckons and teases us. I have played ducks and drakes with it, wasting effort on whims and crazes which should have gone towards projects more worthy. But it has continued to nudge me. And looking back I see that it has been the plumb line that I have used most consistently in building up and running my little business.

Water heating is certainly a problem in a house which has only cold taps. I naturally wanted to have a proper circulation with an immersion heater, but the plumber whom I consulted, knowing that I was only a tenant, did not wish to put me to great expense. He pointed out that the bathroom was not lofty enough to accommodate cistern and tank and did not suggest my having them put, as we did much later, in one of the back bedrooms.

There was, however, gas, a service that I took more or less for granted. In truth I should have been very unwilling to take the house without its aid for cooking, though in Anglesey we had indeed used paraffin which we had found both sensitive and reliable.

The gas people were most helpful especially one old gentleman who had a second-hand basin geyser to dispose of. At first we tried it for washing up but it dribbled along so slowly that its final product was not really hot enough, so after a year or two it was dispatched to the newly refurbished bathroom.

When I first met it this apartment was truly depressing. The bath was metal, white once, now a vague brown in the bottom with copious green water marks below the one tap. The window was covered with red and green patterned paper which allowed no light to penetrate and the 'loo' had a rusty cylinder up aloft. That was all for there was no wash bowl, so we had to buy one of enamel to span one end of the bath. It bore the name 'Posh wash-basin' in black letters. With a compulsion truly Johnsonian in its power I found I had to repeat this appellation every time I went up there. Even painting it out with white paint had little effect.

And this was not the only painting I did for the miserable bath needed two coats of enamel to make it presentable and thereafter a coat each spring to keep it so.

But I have forgotten my friend the gas again for in one corner we found a tap and ring. Mr Hughes, our faithful carpenter, made a strong bracket on which we perched a half-sized washing boiler brought from Lancashire. This had to be filled under the tap and tipped for emptying. The place seemed in fact truly palatial when it was succeeded by a full-sized boiler with inlet pipe and tap. We endured this primitive equipment for many years as the cubic capacity of the bathroom was not sufficient to make a bath geyser safe. This way of heating a bath reminded me of my cousin's house in Kashmir, but there a wood fire had to be lit under the boiler. Our boiler filled the little room first with fumes and then with steam, but it had one good

17

feature. One could, if one left some water in it, wash one's hair in the bath and rinse it very comfortably under its handy tap.

In a few years the bathroom changed its face considerably. My sister foresaw that wartime would bring all sorts of shortages so, just in time, we had a modern bath and lavatory installed and found room for a proper wash bowl with its attendant tiny geyser. A curtain in the corner still hid brushes and mops till one day it caught the geyser pilot light and ended in flames. It was succeeded by a useful cupboard.

Meanwhile water-boiling downstairs was done by kettles on the gas until, after the war, I found a small electric storage heater. During teatime there was little hot water to spare so a supply was stored in large pans in a hay box. This bulky gadget used nowadays only by girl guides and I believe by the economical Scot for making his morning porridge, is surprisingly efficient. It also makes an excellent rat's nest. This I discovered when I returned to the house one spring. Fortunately the occupant was dead and dried up. I think the rats were attracted because the lady next door kept hens in her back garden. I mention them here because the thought of them takes me back better than anything else to a picture of the depressing back regions of the house I had light-heartedly taken on.

If, however, the 'usual offices' were such as to daunt anyone with a small bank balance, technological aids being at their now almost forgotten pre-war level, the same could not be said, with the exception of the bathroom, for the first floor. Four straight forward bedrooms divided the area and the two small back rooms retained their pleasant Georgian style windows. Changes in style percolate slowly to remote districts and some houses in the village escaped Victorian modernisation. Mine at the front did not, so the windows had four large panes only, but they looked south east onto the glorious open view across the Estuary.

One bedroom was immediately designated the sitting room and received the large comfortable winged chair no longer needed at home, a divan bed, a glorious oak mule chest and a padded window seat. The fact that this was made from a suitcase for which my much-travelled sister had offered me half-a-crown made it no less welcome. I had made a green pleated cover for it and padded the top with the contents of unwanted cushions. Curtain material was, of course, folk weave as befitted the period and had been turned out when we had moved to a smaller house. But at least everything being in soft greens and occasionally faded browns went tolerably well together

Its furnishings have changed with the years as a result of visits to antique shops and I have always been so fond of this room that I seem to have been in too great a haste to describe the picture it eventually presented. For indeed the vision that I first had of it was very different.

The floors here and everywhere in the house were covered with a patchwork of oilcloth. Ripping this up was an easy matter and bits of it proved useful for lighting fires in the cast-iron sitting room grate. However the operation left behind a rash of nail heads and it seems that ours was a common experience. Some people who modernised shop-living-premises in Anglesey told me that the nail population on their stairs alone ran into hundreds.

We found that tedious dentistry with the pincers was necessary to render our crop innocuous, but some were obstinate and several whacks of the hammer had to be used to send them home. Oil stain was afterwards put on, followed by polish. Only then did we find how many nails had escaped us and, skulking in corners or still standing under our noses, waited their chance to catch at duster and mop. But how lucky I was to have wood floors everywhere except in the kitchen. Mine is the only house along the little front which has escaped a tiled hall.

Roses festooned the bedroom walls, in some cases several layers of them. The only thing possible was to have the loosest and dampest paper removed and the walls covered with distemper. It is hard to realise that in those not so distant days there was no emulsion paint. Distemper was in fact quite a luxury in those parts, ceilings were often done by amateurs using the decorator's nightmare, whiting.

The two decorators who were sent on the job were cheerful and ready to do their best, but they knew a good deal more about old property than I did. When, a few years later, I asked their boss to come and make a good job of the house; he refused for he knew that as it stood the fabric was not worth it.

It was plain that the men themselves thought little of the house and considered me a mild sort of fool to be attempting to make it presentable. An expert thumb rubbed along the ceilings and they knew the worst. It was no use putting anything on top of the whiting, as it would merely flake off. So the offending surface had to be washed thoroughly or papered after a preliminary rub down. Fortunately some of them had escaped the whiting brush so things were not as bad as they caused me to fear at first.

In thus putting a slightly tragic mask on things like this the decorators were only running to local form. Over and over again in Wales we have asked for service and encouragement, only to be met with a reluctant negative. Then after a little persuasion the sun seems to have come out and the request has been granted with unlooked-for additional favours. Heaped up and running over has been the kindness received, first, however, there must be importunity but importunity tempered with a smile.

This native kindness soon got the better of the men and they gave me several tips. For I was working alongside them on occasion; the £10 allowance made by the owner could not possibly cover all that needed to be done, so I had to do a good deal myself. When using gloss paint you 'brush it on and brush it off' they said, whereas in the case of distemper you 'put it on and leave it on'. They showed me how to work methodically in foot squares never touching up the old work, for the walls of the hall were brown to dado height, so there was a fair acreage to cover. I learnt from them the rule about the consistency of wall paint; it should be such that the surface 'sucked it off the brush'.

I remembered their excellent advice when I was using plastic paint on the wall for the inevitable decorating, without which a house used by so many people would very soon look shabby. From a practical lesson I can profit but I have an inbred aversion to reading directions. My way is to plunge into the work the minute I get the materials home, later to learn, if ever, the correct methods from bitter experience.

For the tea-rooms I chose some delightful cream and ivory papers. Here again sad experience was my tutor, for they faded, marked and showed the damp so that after a few years they had to be treated with special waterproofing solution, then covered with distemper.

I did not tackle all the dark paint at first, it was a big enough job to make the walls presentable so I had to endure brown skirting boards and window and door frames, putting off dealing with these till later. I always worked on this plan when opening the house in the spring. Instead of wearing myself out trying to do a complete spring clean in a few days, I believed in making the place look more or less ready. Then in the lulls that inevitably came after the hectic few days of Easter, I could finish off the details bit by bit. Other people work in other ways. We all need, I think, to find the one that suits us best.

So, apart from a score of unsatisfactory features, my little house was beginning to remind me of the only word of praise that our school art mistress had ever permitted herself. When our group of cubes, pyramids and balls really appeared as if it was standing on a table and not trying to roll uphill; and when the drapery behind it looked like velvet and not a piece of stiff taffeta she would say, "Yes, that's coming." I certainly felt that the house was 'coming' though I did not realise at the time how far it would have to go before I should be satisfied with it.

The dark paint needed constant dusting, and though I had finished the painting of the sign I had to arrange for the erection of a support to display it, and matting had to be put down on the tea-rooms and stairs, and carpet made to go as far as possible upstairs. These jobs done and the doors removed from the tea-rooms, which could at last be set out with the spindle-backed chairs standing round the well-polished tables it all began to look more like the café of my dreams.

Tea things had been ordered from Stoke-on-Trent for the other house. They were specially painted for me in graduated bands of green and were like some that I had admired for sale at Ann's café. And for two winters now I had been searching the junk shops for pewter tea pots. For I knew I should find my café some day and I intended to be prepared. Many were blackened with disuse and had to be cleaned with metal polish mixed with scouring powder. One of the first that I bought was described to me as 'Roman lamp shape'. This, however, means that it is the shape of a very flat tomato. I used it only occasionally, because it was difficult to shake out the tea leaves completely without a great deal of rinsing. The other drawback was that, its surface being, on account of the shape, very large in proportion to the volume of liquid it holds the tea cools quickly. I had some lucky finds however in those early years including two which a knowledgeable friend has pronounced as Queen Anne and another of squarish Georgian shape. With its wooden handle, if it were made in silver it could be dated about 1810. The pewter copies must be dated later. But this would not be one of the copies made in Victorian times when old shapes were repeated and called 'antique pattern'. I have several of these; collected more recently. They are often almost completely round, the lid continuing the unbroken line of the globe. Good Queen Anne shapes, they give away their Victorian origins by their metal instead of ebony handles.

My mother always said that pewter teapots made the best tea. The metal, however, is not the same as that used for the old tankards and trenchers. Many of mine were hard enough to take plating and some were plated when I bought them. The pewter they are made of has a composition of a little copper, about four times as much antimony and ten times as much again of tin.

You pay far more for them now than I did in the thirties, for the Scandinavians have 'found' them. Whereas years ago you could buy them for two shillings now you would find yourself with a very poor specimen for as many pounds. The shopkeeper's patter has changed too. In the old days when you drew a blank he would infuriatingly say to you "You should have come in last week. I sent six to be melted down." Now it is, "What a pity you weren't in yesterday – I sold all I had, to go to Sweden." Nowadays they are costly to buy and just as costly to have buffed and repaired, but how good they look when done, and though they may occasionally get dinged, yet, if you accidentally drop them, they do not break.

Many of the chairs I bought were blackened with varnish. The edge of a penny scraped this off as well as anything, so the junk-shop owners told me. I bought four from the men who collected in the country districts of Lancashire. They then cleaned up the chairs and repaired them for the dealers who called from time to time to pick through their finds. I found no great gems among the chairs that I had collected, but it was exciting to see how the wood grain appeared, ash, cherry, apple wood, when the scraped chair was washed and rubbed with oil. I knew them almost by name after the work I had put into them and they seemed to me and to some of my early customers, a goodly company.

For now at last the sign was up; and a tiny trickle of people began to come into the café. It was mid July 1937.

The mornings kept me busy with baking and preparing our midday dinner in the poorly equipped kitchen. A handful of coffee customers is all I had. In the afternoons we often had no one at all, so, after a stint of painting upstairs, a job that seemed to go on for ever, we would sit quite frankly waiting for customers and gazing at our wonderful view. Nine people for tea one day and we felt really busy, thirty-three and we were rushed off our feet. I say 'we' but I cannot remember who, besides my sister, helped me in that first half season, though the daughter of the friend who had first introduced us to the Anglesey café, certainly came to help and stayed some weeks.

It was serving evening coffee that really got us known. This was certainly something new and as the August evenings drew in a little, people began to come to us for an evening drink. Soon we were serving forty and fifty a night. A resident who, with his wife, ran a small guest house procured excellent coffee for me and also supplied me with tea as he had contacts, having worked in Assam. It was he who gave me the wrinkle of blending a fine-flavoured tea with a strong quick-brewing one. For people like their tea to look strong while tasting interesting.

We soon became well known for our coffee and tea, and some of our earliest customers were the local people. They came first to sample our afternoon tea and soon they were joining the crowds for evening coffee. In the treatment that I received from the Welsh people my experience was very different from what I have heard of many who have started businesses in the southwest. I was never treated as an unwanted foreigner. And yet perhaps this welcome was not so much characteristic of the Welsh, as of the district. The little town near to us was only established about 1820 and many of the good things that have come to it, in a way even its very existence, have been due to the efforts of outsiders. This was true in the early days. The Welsh people often behave as though it is still true today. They sometimes indeed tend to welcome the newcomer more heartily than he subsequently proves to deserve. I hope I deserved the welcome they accorded to me.

After the short summer was over I stayed till the middle of October, though on some days I sold nothing but a brown loaf. My sister had gone back to Lancashire, I had hardly had time to get to know even my neighbours, and occasionally when I came in from an evening walk and when the wind moaned down the hillside behind I felt quite lonely. But the little house held me. As a customer said to me many years later, "it is a happy little house". There was much to do, it was all novel and it was my own place. So I set to work to finish off the back bedrooms ready for friends to stay next year. Curtains had to be made and dressing tables contrived from bed heads resting on boxes. One of the rooms was all in yellow and white spots which I had found at sixpence a yard, and the carpet was green. I thought it was wonderful.

I found, too, that at the end of the season people would enquire for bed and breakfast. Then my little house really could be used and I enjoyed the company.

It was indeed part of a definite plan to stay open fairly late in the season. I realised that if the hotels were still open there must be people about. In time they would surely find me and then being the only café open, I should have the late trade all to myself. It also gave the local people, many of whom are busy in the summer, a chance to patronise me. The experiment was very successful and I found that sales were often good at this time, especially to the honeymooners! Also I myself enjoyed it, for some of the best weather often comes to Wales in October. I can do some gardening before opening in the morning and often a picnic lunch on the beach or in the garden is more pleasant then, than on a blustery day in June. And I had time to talk to people, many of whom were old customers. It took time, of course, for it to become known that I was open late in the season and the first few Octobers were very quiet.

Once the first season was over I began to clear the jungle that was to be the garden and the next spring I could hardly wait till Mr Hughes had sawn through the dividing wall of what was to become the big tea room. For the new back portion I chose a pale Adam green paper and painted the wall cupboards to match. In front of the little black grate I put a tall chest of drawers bought at a local sale room. This was a truly dreadful object brush-grained with bulbous legs and a widely projecting top. However, Mr Hughes sawed off this ugly fringe making the top flush with the sides and boxed in the terrible bulbs with plywood. Painted a greeny grey it looked fine. An ottoman from home took its place against the opposite wall. Its pleated cover and cushion top were green and on the wall behind it I hung cushions, yellow, green and brightly striped, an idea that I had taken from a magazine. They were much admired, especially by the people who were convinced that they were work bags for sale, and tried to take them down from the wall.

The pretty window at the back of the room looked onto a shabby black-painted shed which had been used for coal. Even when this had been dismantled and its assorted contents burnt and otherwise disposed of the earth, where it had stood, was sour and sterile, so at first little could be persuaded to grow. Foxgloves, however, kindly invaded us and a tree lupin, which I had found, was encouraged to spread and cover as much space as possible. It was pleasant to be able to look out on at least the beginnings of a garden.

Several friends and relations came to stay and to help that year and we began to serve more people for tea, which I was more interested in doing than coffee. I had also ordered more things to sell and had the pleasure of arranging them as I wanted. There was little in the garden to bring indoors, but fortunately an enormous variety of wild flowers was at hand with which to fill the vases. I made good use of elm fruits, newly opening pink buds of sycamore, glorious sprays of opening beech leaves and later wild rhododendrons in a surprisingly wide range of shades. These were collected on evening walks and on Sundays when we explored the countryside.

People were kind in giving me flowers too as they could see how much use I had for them. One day when the wife of my landlord came for coffee I had a lovely bowl of nasturtiums arranged naturally with their foliage and twisting growth. She and her husband had a wonderful garden, but had never offered me anything from it. So, when she admired the nasturtiums I let her know that I had found them thrown on a heap not far from her gate. All that came was grist to my mill for the time being.

The Sunday closing was not resented so much then as it was later when the Welsh keeping of Sunday became a little less strict. I took the idea over, like so many others, from the café on Anglesey, knowing that I should need to have one day of rest. The decision proved a wise one. As the Welsh people had been so kind I saw no point in offending them by introducing a secular Sunday into their midst.

Funnily enough it was the old-established visitors who were most critical of me, though I did not realise at the time how carefully I ought to be watching my step. I found this out some years later when two sisters informed me that in those early years my presence was slightly 'resented'. It was their word. However they apparently bravely came to see what the place was like, reported to one another that, after all, their holiday village was perhaps not going to be spoilt, and decided it would be safe to patronise me.

That winter my sister Fanny went to stay in Bombay and I went off to do a pottery course for six weeks. I greatly enjoyed it. As a result I can talk fairly knowledgeably about some of the processes involved in pottery making. I know, for example, what slipware is and that it is not 'slipper ware' as one customer described it. More and more people are learning to make pottery and they enjoyed looking at hand-made pieces with someone who can tell them how some of the effects are obtained.

If I may digress for a moment I would mention a quite important discovery that I made during the pottery course. As a rest from throwing, my teacher suggested that I should paint some tiles. I had done no drawing since leaving school where I usually managed to be amongst the top six in the form. My early failure with tile-painting had a result that surprised me, for I could not toss it off and say, "no, not my line". It made me moody, touchy and almost tearful. I knew enough of child psychology, from helping in a little boarding school, to know that there must be a reason for this apparent 'naughtiness'. Later I realised what it was. For where there is no ambition, failure does not hurt. The experience showed me that after two summers in the loveliness of Wales, I desperately wanted to draw. So when I had some time to spare in the years that followed I went out and had a go. I am still doing it though I do not find it, as others are reputed to do, relaxing. Quite the reverse in fact, though wonderfully engrossing and satisfying.

Another thing I learnt at the Pottery was to use two hands for a job. It is surprising how often we are content to be only 'dextra dextrous'. I once saw a student icing a cake with her left hand held against the small of her back. It was a mannerism that my father had when taking up the church collection. Using both hands all day it was with him probably an unconscious acknowledgement of the joy of the Sunday holiday. It amused me to see the familiar habit practised by someone else, but I pointed out that in housework the left hand usually has an important job to do.

Another household motto with us is 'never go empty-handed'. There is often something to be carried to the place you are making for if it is put down in a 'popping spot'. One of our 'popping spots' is on the stairs for things are always needing to be carried up. It also tends to be my place for newspapers which I have not finished reading. One week I had five part-read newspapers mounting the stairs between the banisters. I only realised how odd, also how untidy they must have looked, when someone asked if they were for sale!

Before tackling my first complete season we went in the early spring of 1938 to Garmisch. The intention was that I should learn to ski but I never really succeeded in hauling the heavy skis up the nursery slopes, so we turned it into a sight-seeing holiday. We happened to go to Innsbruck on the day of the Anschluss when a party of German soldiers marched into the city. In place of bayonets they bore on their shoulders new, highly polished spades. Little did we realise that in two years' time they would be attempting to dig the grave of free Europe.

The next spring of 1939 brought my sister home from India again and it brought also the help and amusing company of a Swiss girl, Lina. When she had time to spare from the children she came down to me. She loved helping with the evening coffees, by now enough to keep us very busy. Her energy was truly inexhaustible and when after ten o'clock I was washing up with one eye half closed she would be still full of gusto and would put on the gramophone waking us all up with 'Mad Dogs and Englishmen'.

A musical college friend with equal energy came to stay that summer. They walked me for miles and amazed me with the quantity of Beethoven they could sing. The violin concerto was their favourite for this purpose. One of our jaunts was to go part by 'bus and part on foot to the Italianate village of Portmeirion, clambering in by the back way after braving a field where a bull was ranging. We would then proceed to lose ourselves on the tortuous paths that led down to that delectable beach.

One evening Lina and I decided to row across the estuary and see how this charming village looked from the water. We could both handle a boat and choosing, as we thought, the right time for the tide we reached the other shore quite easily. It had, however, taken rather longer than we had allowed and on the way back the tide began to carry us seawards. We pulled hard for what seemed a very long time and at last reached the shelter of the bay. There we arrived panting, hot and blistered to find three of the local sea captains watching out for us at the point. Trying to put as good a face on things as possible, I said to one of them, "we were caught by the tide." "Of course you were," he replied, "but we'd have sent someone out after you if there had been any danger."

Pilot Holding used to take us out rowing and on one occasion he had a disturbing tale to tell. Some years before a local family who owned a cabin cruiser had been entertaining some German visitors. The Germans liked nothing better than sailing in the estuary and on one occasion when their host could not accompany them the pilot was asked to act as skipper. "I had occasion," said Pilot Holding, "to go down to the cabin and found it locked," he said, "and me, the skipper, not allowed to go in. I've a pretty good idea of what they were doing there." When after the war the German maps were exhibited locally and showed that ours was the estuary chosen for the invasion, I thought back to Pilot Holding's story.

There were in the village at that time, five or six sea captains who had been masters of ships built in the estuary. I was fascinated by the history of these old sailing ships but little guessed then how my interest in them would involve me in the defence of a copyright, but so it turned out.

I was to learn, among other things, that the master of one of these little vessels would, if he found himself in Leghorn, stop a few days to have the ship's portrait painted. Thereafter it hung with pride for many years on the parlour wall at home.

All this and much more about fish and phosphate carriers was told some years later in a book, *Immortal Sails*, written by Henry Hughes, a son of one of the port's seafaring families. His brother helped by collecting, for the illustrations, photos of the ships' portraits, taken in any house in which he could still track them down. It was partly a labour of love for many of the portraits had by this time been relegated to cellar and attic whence they are only now being unearthed. In the process he made a large scrap-book, kept in the National Library of Wales, in which he entered details of crews and voyages when these could be ascertained.

While he was compiling it he had the idea of tinting one of his photographs which he framed and gave to me to hang in the hall, as he felt that people might be interested.

They certainly were and, as many of them wanted to buy it, I asked him if he thought it could be reproduced. Without thinking to consult the owner of the original, Mr Jones, who was still living quite near, we decided that the best plan would be to have a block made from the photo and to use it to print my very own 'souvenir ware'.

This was to be all the easier as I knew the designer of the firm who painted my tea cups. They, amongst other things, did the type of printing very pleasantly in colour. I was quite excited about the little venture. Only when I had begun to sell the beakers, ashtrays and teapot stands and had an account of the ship and her sad end written in italics for the interested purchaser to read, did the owner of the original picture remark to Mr Hughes that he was not quite sure whether he approved of the idea.

Mr Hughes however mollified him by saying that I was not really intending to make a great deal of money out of what was, after all, his property because the pots would only be sold in my place and to people who were genuinely interested. Many people who came in fact to buy pieces were descended from the ship's builders or from someone who had sailed in her.

So far so good, but a few years later the pottery that printed for me was sold and with it, of course, the designs in use. I knew the purchasers of the firm and asked them if they would continue to print for me from my block. I never thought to point out to them that to save expense, it had been printed on a large block with several others and it was in fact my property.

After a few years they suddenly announced that they could no longer take on the work. So I arranged that another firm, for whom the designer I had known was now working, should borrow the block when necessary and do my printing for me. After a time they made objections to this arrangement because, they said, they were constantly needing other designs which were on the large block. Still I took no alarm and the designer quietly had the block copied so that we need not trouble them further. One spring we happened to be looking round the Port and found a new craft shop stocked to the roof with assorted goods including ash-trays jumbo cups and tankards all decorated with my ship design.

I was amazed. So also were many of my local customers, some of whom even received from friends pieces which had been bought as far away as Devon and Cornwall. They were obviously hurt that our picture of our ship built in the bay here, our speciality, should be sold anywhere but at the Bobbing Boats.

Many letters to my solicitor in Manchester, often written late at night, were now required. As a result of these it was decided that I must find out if the picture was still in private hands, Mr Jones having left it to his daughter, Mr Hughes' widow helped me to trace her. She in turn reassured me that the original was in her house and she had no objection to the use I was making of its reproduction. Armed with this information, Counsel was at last able to pronounce that, as it constituted a work of art, I had a copyright in the block.

The pottery probably did not mind. They had made their money out of it and the legal costs had to be borne by me.

But as I saw it a principle was involved, and, having, by that time a little more money than when I started, I was willing to face the expense of defending it. That the running of a small craft shop in the way I thought it should be run, would involve me in this sort of thing, I little guessed when, so long ago we used to talk to the captains of those old sailing ships. The son of one of them wore gold ear-rings which we were told served as a sort of bank book if he should be shipwrecked. He was lost without hope of rescue in the war that descended on us that September.

And with that war came evacuees both government-sponsored and private. I had the hardest five summers of my life trying to serve them. Little knowing that our estuary was the one chosen by Hitler for his projected invasion, people came with their families feeling that it was one of the places where they could be safe.

The PewterTeapots – a sketch by Mary Howe

Chapter II

Getting Going

God helps those who help themselves Benjamin Franklin

Early in the war rationing came along and we were introduced to what was known in the local Food Offices as the 'Bassick' quantity. For it was based on an amount of provisions that one had used before the war. As I was a new beginner, my 'Bassick' was never adequate. I was chronically short of fat and sugar. Recipes were whittled down till they were barely recognisable so that each piece of cake should require only one twelfth of an ounce of fat. The points system, which many of us have almost forgotten, came to the rescue, however, because for every hundred meals served a café qualified for a certain number of points. With these syrup and dried fruit could be bought. The addition of syrup can make a very plain cake taste quite rich and good.

Besides this allowance which was intended for manufacturing, we also had a fat and sugar allocation which depended on the number of meals we served. A record had to be kept of every meal and hot drink and returned to the Food Office each month. A rumour went round to the effect that a tea could be counted as a meal as well as a hot drink, since most people drank more than one cup. Whether this really was so I never enquired, but hoped for the best and filled in my 'returns' accordingly.

Once or twice when I had to refuse extra jam a certain customer would say in a knowing way, "do you need to be so short?" I could probably have had help but did not wish to get involved. More than once in fact the wholesale suppliers helped out because some cafés with a large 'bassick' of sugar could not use it all. So we were confidentially told of supplies that were 'not taken up'. By this means a tiny trickle of extra sugar found its way into my tins. I was never lucky with extra fat.

It was a terrible feeling, but most people were wonderfully understanding. The most difficult ones were refugees of Teutonic origin. Someone must have told them that in the first war Wales had been, comparatively, a land of plenty. They could not be convinced that rationing this time was more efficient and they continued to ask for boiled eggs when the docile English understood that such things were not to be had.

Compared with that of the towns our milk ration was fairly flexible so people on holiday from the bombs flocked in for coffee. A situation which arose from milk rationing made me unpopular with the local people for a time. I knew that their men were in the forces and were facing great dangers on the high seas as captains and engineers of merchant ships. They themselves, however, were living comparatively quiet lives compared with women in some of the cities. So when local girls began to come every evening for coffee I asked them if they would ration themselves to two or three times a week, to leave room and milk for the visitors. The story soon went around that I was unwilling to serve Welsh people. This is the only unkindness I have suffered at their hands. I was very worried about the food situation and working a good deal of the time under strain and I took it very hard. However I continued to be frank and the matter was soon forgotten.

One English family staying at a smart hotel nearby used to come for tea fortified with a tin of syrup. They probably had extra bread with them too. I thought how very wise they were. It was the small boys sent to the kitchen door, plate in hand, with the cheerful request, "Do you think we could have some more bread and butter?" who tried my patience most. But I often managed to produce the extra for them.

What seemed the last straw was the rationing of flour. I got over this by putting a begging bowl in the hall into which people kindly popped their spare coupons. When I told the Food Office of my bright idea they said I was breaking the law, but, needless to say, nothing happened.

I had no help with the waiting though my aunt's housekeeper kept us going with the washing-up. She loved to help in the evenings too. I often carried tea to eighty people in an afternoon. At the and of it, my back aching, I could go through them all, table by table, remembering the jokes and the near spills as well as the queue of people in the hall, many of them reading their books while they patiently waited their turn. It certainly felt worthwhile.

In spite of the worry of rationing I realised that I was lucky to be doing work that I loved in a safe place, work too that I felt to be purposeful. Many people have told me since what those wartime teas meant to them. And apart from occasional streptococcal infections in my throat, which my doctor treated with great patience and resource, I seemed to keep in good health.

By the early summer of 1941 it was obvious that we should have to extend the kitchen. My aunt's friend came up with the best idea but I was unwilling to spend the money as I did not own the house. The long west-facing wall was becoming damper than ever and the bathroom was a constant annoyance. So, judging that my landlord might not now be able to carry out his schemes behind the house I hoped that he might instead be willing to realise on it. So I wrote to ask him and he invited me to go and see him.

I knew of Mr Chivers by hearsay and I was not too sanguine of the result of our meeting. In the village he was known as a very astute business man. Like all newcomers he had been welcomed on his first arrival. However his habit of buying up land and property in the district was making people a little apprehensive. They wondered what he intended to do with it. One cottage that he had bought, however, he refused to part with and on this account I was inclined to admire him.

For the cottage straddled the spot where the steep road, leading out of the village, turned into a footpath. After a few hundred yards this joined another road. If he could be persuaded to sell land here the road could be driven straight through and the peace of the village would be lost for the future. As I had chosen Borth-y-Gest partly because it was, like the Anglesey village, a cul-de-sac, I hoped it would remain so for many years to come.

Mr Chivers opened the interview with a long story of his losses in the Midlands where he was interested in several industrial undertakings. It seemed that at one of his factories he was in a similar position to mine. His landlord, however, was a local authority. He ended his tale of woe by snapping his fingers in the air as he said, "And they won't do a thing for me." It struck me as slightly comic that

34

this man who could have 'bought me out' fifty times over should be thus moaning over his bad luck to me. I saw him as the type who might be ruthless in success, yet who resorted to self pity if things went against him. But his own pity was enough; he did not want mine. From me he expected as tough an exterior as he himself normally showed to business opponents. So I showed it.

When my turn came I said, "Yes, Mr Chivers, and I have a landlord too." Then I added, snapping my fingers on the operative word as he had done "and he won't do a thing for me". It was done before I had really had time to think, and I awaited results with some apprehension. But I had judged him aright. He smiled and softened immediately and before long the house was mine. I was to pay nearly twice what he had given for it four years before, but though the fabric was poor, I knew that the site would always be valuable.

Such modest success as this, was not however, reflected at first in the realm of 'personnel'. When my aunt left the village in 1944 I found her housekeeper impossible to replace. We might now have a larger and more modern kitchen but we were very far from finding anyone to staff it. We were, however, a little less busy in the café and I tried the experiment of having young helpers who would do a little of the kitchen work as well as helping in the tea rooms.

With the first ones I did not seem to be lucky. I have found in running the café that any innovation has worked badly at first, for almost long enough sometimes, to suggest my giving it up. Only with the persistence which is more akin to obstinacy, have I been able to reap a crop of success from new ideas. Some of the early mistakes were probably partly my own fault and in spite of them I have been exceedingly lucky and I have learnt some amusing and inspiring things about people.

One spring I had quite a personable young student to help me. As she was on her own I felt responsible for her entertainment, yet could not always go out with her. One quiet morning I suggested that she should walk along the sea edge and pick some primroses for the little bowls on the tea tables. "But I should be followed," she said.

I cannot remember my amazed reply. It was probably in the nature of "Good Heavens, who by?" I neither expected nor received an

35

answer, but decided that I should have to do my own primrose picking in future.

If she gave me a nasty surprise my odd house on one occasion returned the compliment. One cold Sunday she had been kneeling by the sitting room fire not realising that we had had a false front of cream asbestos fixed to cover the black cast-iron and had also added a loose shelf. Putting her hand on this shelf to help herself up she found the whole contraption coming down on top of her. Pots and clock rolled in all directions, but nothing was broken. As one of my customers who rented the house from me one war winter always used to say, "we had to laugh".

If I had wondered who might follow this girl on her walks the mother of another young helper could have informed me without hesitation. For when she was taking a cup of coffee before leaving her daughter with me, she embarked on the subject of white slave traffic. It was quite obvious to her that the cliff paths of Borth-y-Gest were haunted by skilled procuresses, or would they be procurateurs? I was too amazed to ask and hastily changed the subject, promising at the same time to take every care of the girl. She was sweet and sensible and I wondered if she had any idea what phantoms of worry were filling her mother's head.

Another mother actually took rooms in the village while her daughter H was with me. A sister on leave from the WRNS also came. I remarked with relief how lovely it was for them to be here as they could spend H's free time together. This was, it seems, to take a too frivolous view of affairs for Mama replied, "I have only come to chaperone H." As H delighted in talking to gentlemen out of the upstairs window, I felt that her mother was really wasting her time.

However I soon found that her mother's metier lay in another direction. She wanted to help in the café. So after a few days she insinuated herself in the person of a floor usher, posted at the end of the hall. She imagined that her duties were done when she had taken a vague order and passed it on to the slaves in the kitchen. I, however, viewed things differently and got her buttering bread. This she named the 'spreading performance' and as it was not so much to her taste we soon found that her other daughter needed her company, if not her surveillance, in the afternoon, so we got rid of her.

If we owed her nothing else we are at least indebted to her for a word in our private vocabulary. For if I do not care for a job, or if it seems to take more effort and time than I feel is justified, I tend to call it a 'performance'. Many jobs come into this category, such as dusting the high plate shelf and washing its occupants, but they have to be done occasionally.

After these early encounters with the sex-obsessed, I was luckier. The rest of my helpers have either had a normal attitude towards men or else, revelling in their single blessedness they have considered them as virtually non-existent. And we had in those early days true romance too. One of a pair of sisters, who came for the whole summer, met her husband here, a keen tennis player like herself. A literature student of whom I was very fond came more than once. She had a great capacity for falling in and out of love, but she was in love with life and with everything and also had a great sense of humour. As she had no mother I enjoyed the role of elder sister and confidante. She eventually married the man to whom she had really given her heart before I knew her. We talked about everything, dressmaking, poetry and music as well as Catholicism, about which she taught me a good deal. I often surprise my many Catholic helpers with my knowledge as a result. We spent hours in the sitting room with the gramophone. She especially liked the slow movement of Grieg's Piano Concerto and when the tide was up to the sea wall below the window she used to put on the record of Final's Cave. It was she who, in her enthusiasm for life and her strangely mature understanding of its demands and rewards, encouraged me to stick at my painting. For after the usual spell of beginner's luck I had come upon the inevitable difficulties.

Elder sister and confidant was, however, one of the many roles I played in the years after the war. Another was that of cook-housekeeper. For after being so desperately short of help, I went to the other extreme and engaged more help than I really needed.

One year we were five, including a Swedish girl, all living in. With a cooked breakfast and midday dinner as well as some sort of high tea I was kept busy. But I was not doing the work I had intended to do. Though, after the hard grind of wartime I enjoyed the company, the fun and the jokes, I vaguely felt that something was wrong.

Though I could not have put it into words at the time, Parkinson's Law was in charge. The more the household grew the more there was to do. A friend, a little older than me, came two summers, and the washing up, shopping and food preparation provided her with the part-time work she wanted. She was worried about the future and absent-minded. On one occasion after shelling peas she put the edible part in the bin and brought me the pods to cook. She replaced them, of course, but it was all rather a waste of time. On another occasion the kippers for tea could not be found. The larder was, as ever, a dumping spot for everything, and it turned out that someone had picked up the parcel, thinking it was rubbish, and popped it in the bin outside. At the end of a sunny afternoon we found it still there, mercifully on the top but a little high all the same. However, rationing was still on and a kipper was a kipper, so they were salvaged, washed and eaten.

In those after-war years everyone helped with everything including the baking, but I saw less than I wanted to of the café. In fact the story was round the village that I intended to sell it to the Swedish girl, a glorious blond who cooked herself to a chestnut in her spare time; it was the hot summer of 1949.

My spare time was spent in the sitting room window whence I would descend when the afternoon began to get busy. The two pairs of sisters who helped me about that time were so efficient and so keen that they could be left to run the café on their own. Both pairs opened cafés themselves after leaving me, so it was important to give them as much responsibility as possible. Yet they were young and did not know the craft-shop stock well, so I did not feel justified in leaving them and going out. Two of them had been to a good and rather ladylike school in the Midlands and were charming with the customers. They could, however, see the funny side of some of them.

According to them Sunday uniform at, shall we call it 'High Elms', was a tussore dress, white shoes and stockings, white coat and panama hat. One week we had a very regular customer whom they named 'The High Elms Girl', and took turns to serve. At last I made an excuse to investigate and found a little lady of uncertain age wearing a tussore 'costume', an ancient cream-coloured hat and white wrinkly stockings and plimsolls. They had some quiet fun out of her but never betrayed by a muscle that she was their joke of the week.

Some of the other people who helped me about that time hav
me that I was sometimes testy and hard to please. I insiste
example, on matching up cream jugs and sugar bowls and the til
used for teapot stands. The tea things were the same banded d
that we had started with but they were now a warm tan brown.
variety of colours contrasted pleasantly with them, greys, br
greens and turquoise shades. Done as I liked it done, the effect
very pleasant. Mixed up at random every piece lost its value.

I was probably unnecessarily fussy but, as some of the people v
with me for several months, I thought that they could really h
mastered it. If they had taken the trouble they could have worked
the problem for themselves instead of rather grudgingly trying
please me, or just hoping for the best. My occasional fussiness abc
what I considered to be 'artistic' details was the only cause of frictic
that we encountered in all those years. On the whole we seemed to
in very happily. I was lucky to find at least six long-term helpers wh
were as enthusiastic about café-running as I was. They were pleased t
have found a café in which to gain their experience. I was glad to hav
found them. In happy routine the summer sped by; they, sorry to fee
their time at Borth-y-Gest passing so quickly, yet at the same time
planning and looking forward to a place of their own; I, carried along
as I tend to be by the day-to-day life of the place.

Time never hung heavily; there was always so much to be done.
And, older now and perhaps a little more experienced, I learnt
amongst other things that when tired or a little depressed, it is wise not
to survey life in a general way; it will appear far too grey. It is better to
fix on one cheerful facet of it, or if none seems to present itself, then
force oneself to 'count one's blessings'. In the mood of the moment
this will probably not take long, but the attempt seems to release a
bubble of satisfaction which rises and carries one's spirits up with it.

It may be that I am, as one of my school fellows called me, 'one of
the merry ones'. Perhaps it is more true to say that business has been
the tonic I need to take me out of myself, by its constant and pleasant
stimulus. The only time, in fact, when I used to feel flat was when the
evenings drew in at the end of the season, particularly if poor weather
brought a sudden lull in custom. The happy busy house would seem
strangely quiet then, and something seemed to be wrong. Now a

mixture of 'philosophy' and house refurbishing has made this time a good deal happier.

And there is, of course, always the garden. If as usual, it falls below one's expectations and hopes, still, as Kipling knew so well, a time spent wrestling with it if it is not behaving well enough to give us pleasure, can at least send us indoors afterwards feeling more in tune with life. But I realised too that there might be another factor to account for my occasional moodiness. I felt that the place was slipping out of gear: proportion was being lost. I had for several years enjoyed helping to train other people to run cafés. I would now for a change have the fun once more of working actively on my own.

Apart also from helping to give prospective caterers the same kind of help which I have gained in Anglesey, I have been interested to hear of at least two cafés which owed their existence in the first place to having seen mine. I went to have tea at one in Cheshire. The house had been specially built for the purpose and I was shown the beautiful kitchen and was able to admire the immaculate tiled floor. I was not, however, greatly surprised when I heard that, after a spell of years, the owners had decided to sell as they had found the standing too much for them. Probably if I were running a café all the year round my feet would have given in long ago, but I wondered how much the tiled floor had, in this case, contributed to the inevitable tiredness.

To return to my own problems, at this point I decided to try to work with a much smaller staff and the experiment was a success. A part-time helper who lived quite near gave me more of her time. She understood my ways perfectly and she helped to train the students and occasional helpers who filled in at the busy times.

Of these I seemed to find a wonderful variety. There was an air hostess who caught a very bad cold so giving me the excuse of suggesting that the climate did not suit her. For the place did not afford her the scope she needed, so she found a job in Cornwall and found a husband there too. She left her friend behind whose company I enjoyed enormously. She was not the only one who was trying her hand at writing, for another girl who helped me wrote short stories for Canadian magazines. A friend of a friend who helped me had lived *au pair* in Norway where the family went out skiing in swimming togs. After the heat of their house it was probably a form of sauna bath.

I came to think of my place at that time as a sort of junction or marshalling yard where people came when they were thinking of changing their jobs. A teacher came into this category. Obviously unsettled, though cheerful and good company and excellent at the job. She later joined her sister in running a hotel. Another one is still teaching for she came merely for the experience. She has since provided me with welcome help in the shape of two nieces.

There were widows too, bravely settling to a new life or taking a vacation job while in term time providing digs for students. To one of these I was most grateful. She and her husband had owned a small hotel and she showed me how very many jobs could be done sitting down. As a result I now do all my weighing out as well as very many other jobs sitting relaxed on Mrs Ward's stool. A young Austrian girl whose home was a great timber estate had been sent by her mother to one of my friends to learn English. She would tackle anything and was good at dressmaking. That year I found a Liberty tussore dress at the local fair for thirty shillings. She discovered that the middle of the gored skirt had not been put to the middle of the bodice, so altered it for me. She loved the mountains and rode miles on my bicycle. But she was longing all the time for home and her *Hubertus Mantel* and the hunting. My German was not equal to this word so she had to explain that it was a green cloak they wore for hunting, St Hubert being patron of the chase. What a remote world from ours and what a stir she created in her dirndl!

Then there was the ex-customer who had done a Good Housekeeping course. She was large and had to be circumnavigated. But she repaid handsomely in entertainment for any inconvenience her size caused us. At that time I kept under the kitchen table a large gipsy crock which I used for bread-making. It was covered with a starched cloth held taut and secured under the rim by a running of elastic. This she christened the 'dancing floor' and averred that when the kitchen was quiet at night the mice held balls on it. I said we had no mice just then, but she would not be convinced. In any case, she said it would do them no good, for with mice as with humans, it had been decreed that, "you can't get to Heaven on a dancing floor."

Having been a Wren she could no doubt have given us, if we had asked her, a rendering of that other war-time evergreen, "Life gets tedious dunnit?" With her around it certainly had little chance of doing so. And I must not forget the Russian violinist whose parents had escaped with her as a baby, at the time of the Revolution. They had to go by sledge and in spite of the danger from wolves her mother had to run by the sledge from time to time to whip up her circulation and so keep the baby warm. Afterwards she herself had lived in Warsaw, whence she had to escape again in World War II, walking to the home of her father's friends in Hamburg. Being an artist I thought she might have her head in the clouds, but she was completely practical and willing to do everything and I enjoyed helping her with her English.

I had bought a bicycle a few years before this, partly because I had noticed a strange swelling near my diaphragm and I found that the jerking on a long walk upset me, and also I noticed that if I came into a hot room after exertion I had a tearing thirst and felt that my last hour had come. The bicycle gave me fresh air and exercise off my feet and I found some wonderful flat country up the valley with glorious views all round. The rhythm of walking on a smooth road can be wonderfully relaxing, but there is nothing so restful as the quiet tick tick of a bicycle free wheel homeward bound on a summer evening.

I kept away from doctors, as one of my aunts had had to undergo an operation for symptoms similar to mine. At last I was told of a nature-cure specialist in Birmingham and made an appointment to see him.

By that time I had acquired a pre-war Austin car so, by getting up at six and baking the scones before I left, I was able to drive to Gobowen and take the train from there. I had not seen cornfields with poppies in them, or people playing cricket in white flannels for many, many years; in fact I had forgotten what the English countryside looked like in summer, so I revelled in those train journeys. For I had to go every week for nearly two months.

On examination it was found that the muscles that were causing the swelling had hardened around the main aorta and were holding up the blood supply. The treatment was compresses made of vegetable unguents combined with concentrated massage to soften the muscular complex. The masseur told me I had just come in time. If I had been trying to lift anything very heavy in the garden with my blood vessels compressed there might have been fatal results. The cause, he said, was anxiety – most probably anxiety about food supplies, for rationing had continued until 1948 by which time we were serving large numbers and needing a great quantity of cakes. Anxiety can, it seems, take different people in different ways. In some it causes ulcers. I felt that compared with the trouble I should have had with ulcers, I had been let off gently.

This relatively easy interlude when I could go off sometimes for the early afternoon to be back soon after four was only possible because, besides Margaret, I had found Mrs Ward for the washing up. She came when I needed her and for as long as I needed her. So with fewer people to cook for, and less shopping and housework to do I was able to be more in the café. I had enjoyed having a large and happy household, I was now to enjoy, for many years, the luxury of having just the right help, someone in the café as well as on the craft side who was entirely reliable, cheerful, keen and willing and who also knew the stock.

I have had a number of people to help in the kitchen from time to time, but the one who stays most in my mind was Mrs Ward, a Lancastrian of character. I owe her two debts and bless her name many times. For she was of the Benjamin Franklin persuasion and believed in the power that accrues from self help.

From time to time we used to be plagued with mice as old houses in the country often are. Luckily I acquired, when I first arrived, a really efficient break-back trap the like of which is no longer made. With this my aunt one winter caught twenty-two of the little creatures. It was left to Mrs Ward, a 'tackler' if ever there was one, to deal with the problem. She did so by divining with a sort of sixth sense where their holes were and filling them up with a mixture of broken glass and putty. As the spots favoured were often behind the oven the job was a little touch-and-go as the stuff had to be poked into position by means of a stick. My long arm worked under her direction, and afterwards we had peace for many years. The odd visitor that I might hear scratching round in late September could be dealt with by the trap.

Some people, when the delicate subject of mice comes up, claim that theirs are only visitors because they are field mice. They tacitly suggest that there is a great difference in status between the field mouse and the house mouse. The field mouse, according to them, may visit even the most respectable home at harvest time. On the contrary, of the house variety, it seems, you must breed your own; and they can never reflect any credit upon you. According to this doctrine we certainly took a step up when my magic trap held one autumn morning a long-nosed bewildered baby shrew. There must surely be something special about a house in which such a confirmed country-lover can be persuaded to take up residence. The residence would, however, be short in any case in an empty house with food shut carefully away. For a shrew, being fat, has to eat three times its own weight of food to keep alive in cold weather. It would find the thin and energetic mouse's winter diet of paper quite inadequate.

Last year my trap was not to be found. I searched, but in vain. A local shop let us have on approval one of the latest models, a self-setting affair, but I could not make it work. Then out of their archives they produced an old stock one, but that was no use as it went off before I could get it into position. Having no platform, it was difficult to set really fine. Then I remembered. We had had a mouse in the spring in the under-stair cupboard opening from the lobby. Perhaps I had set the trap there. One afternoon Lilian started to investigate and at the same time turn out the sheets of paper and rolls of corrugated cardboard – bound to come in useful some day – that always seemed to fill up what would otherwise be a roomy storage space. While the operation was in progress we erected the movable cupboard door across the lobby for, while these investigations were going on, people were having tea in the café.

We were so absorbed that the customers had to come for hot water, handing the jug over the barricade, and not suspecting, we hoped, the real object of our search. At last floor level was reached. There was the trap, still holding a mummified mouse. I trust that the laughter which greeted it sounded no more than what would morally accompany the satisfying task of autumn cleaning. My other debt to Mrs Ward is 'the stool'. In days gone by I used a folding stool for such tedious jobs as buttering bread. But as old age began to steal over us all we found its aid more and more essential and its shape and frailty less and less acceptable. One spring when I arrived and went to see Mrs Ward, she took me into her kitchen to show me the new stool which her husband had made for us. It was firm and strong and oblong with a handy shelf underneath. At the side there is room to slide the 'second storey'. For the staff is always of two sizes and persuasions. Some like to perch on the stool plus biscuit tin plus cushion, the others sit on the stool and cushion only. But we all agree in deciding that 'the stool', with all the accretions of cushion cover – loose for ease of removal – table dusters, oven cloths, tea towels and anything in fact that anyone may have lost and which has a way of settling on it or near it, is the most in important feature of the kitchen.

Mrs Ward died in 1962 so I have her help no longer. Two years later my local assistant, Margaret, who had helped for over fifteen years took a job in the town. She is the manageress of a shop which is open all through the year. Many people recognising her thought at first that I had started a branch. They were giving me credit for ability I do not possess.

By the time I was left on my own again I found I had regained my cheerfulness and gusto as well as my health so completely that I felt I could face most things with equanimity. After a rather terrifying interlude the staff problem resolved itself once more with the help of a part-time washer-up, an excellent local schoolgirl and a friend Lilian who helps me part-time. The part-time washer-up has however had to give up for health reasons, but just a week before she went into hospital, Fred joined the staff.

The name must have come to me in the night for I woke up saying we had acquired a Revolving Electric Dishwasher. Lilian, more 'with it' than I am, supplied the adjective 'Fabulous', so FRED he is. I had resisted for a long time the idea of an electric dishwasher because I had heard such alarming reports of some of them. I thought too that with draining racks for cups as well as for plates and saucers mechanisation had gone as far as I could take it. And as usual I was apprehensive about space.

However, a customer whose visits I always enjoyed happened to come at just the right time. She is a professional flower arranger who grows her own flowers including glorious orchids. I always feel flattered when she buys containers from me. She told me that, with a business to run, and a husband to look after, she had decided that something must be done about the household chores. So she had taken the plunge and now she was sure that the model she had decided on would be suitable for me and, most importantly, would fit into my space.

Fred does not do everything. You have to stack him and turn him on and off and I usually overlook one detail of procedure either by omitting the rinsing or forgetting to insert the powder. But he is undoubtedly a great help. All the cups have to be soaked first however, for he has no interest in tea and coffee stains. So having accustomed ourselves to one rhythm and one set of equipment we are now having to study another. But I think it will be worth it for half the battle with small scale catering is work study.

I have never had any professional advice in this line, preferring to use my own head. Perhaps seeing a kitchen on which a friend had spent a three-guinea advice fee and in which the cups were hung separately on hooks shook my confidence. The kitchen had every other gadget imaginable but those hooks struck me as a very odd idea. We hardly ever put cups away, but instead have four trays always ready and as the clean crocks come to hand the trays are set with them.

My kitchen is certainly not a gadget paradise for I only like the gadgets that do a job without creating another one, and do it well. If I could find something that would chop walnuts leaving them crisp, not mashed up like flour, I would buy it tomorrow. And I really must get a wall tin-opener. I have an automatic tea caddy but it unfortunately upsets our arithmetic by measuring out the tea in coffee spoons. Still, we use it quite often. Of all the things for which we have to thank the scientists my memory of thirty years in and out of the kitchen never fails to remind me. Detergents, so much pleasanter and more thorough than soap, and non-stick milk pans – how I bless mine! Stainless steel and black enamel casseroles in which to cook the vegetables and bring them to table. And what did we do without polythene bags?

But all these details are a little dreary. They are, however, a part of café running that the enthusiasts tend to overlook. I could not count the number of women, married as well as single, who have confessed to me a secret disappointment that they have never been able to achieve their ambition of running a small café.

I agree that it is a delightful job but the pots are always with us and the washers-up are not. I once exchanged notes with the owner of a café in the Cotswolds. She told me that she always arranged to have what she called 'two lines of defence' between herself and the risk of having to do the cooking. My Maginot line, if I could have one, would be firmly fixed round the kitchen sink.

And yet one's disposition can help a good deal in softening some of the rough edges of café work. If you cannot go out nor have a meal until the sink is clear, you are probably in for a hard grind. For in a café there is, as in many art galleries, a 'permanent collection' and it is as well to learn to live with it. Better far to leave some pots unwashed if the sun is shining and go out. You will come back relaxed and invigorated by the fresh air and the job will seem to be done in half the time. At least that has been my experience. On Sundays after a week of strict tidiness I let myself go completely and the kitchen table looks like the one in the film *I'm All Right Jack* when the shop steward's wife had gone on strike and he is left to manage. You can't put a pin between the things. But it all serves to remind me that it is indeed Sunday.

I probably make things no easier for myself by not being very good at accepting friendly help at odd times. I have often had friends to stay in the quiet part of the season and let them jog on at the odd jobs in their own way so that we could go out together. Others have helped me while Margaret has had a few days' holiday. They have worked like Trojans for in a few days a newcomer can get to know how things are done and where things are kept. It is the odd help at busy times that has to be gratefully refused and those who offer it usually understand. When you are in a rush you are least able to put a stranger into the way of things and extra inert bodies have to be walked round.

Recently two friends helped us out of a 'jam' at very short notice. We were two people short in early August. They were staying nearby for several weeks so I told them of our plight. They said they would be only too delighted to help. They worked very hard and very efficiently and much fun was had by all. Of course we talked hard through it all and one customer looking for some beads at the end of the afternoon had to come into the kitchen to find me. I apologised for not having heard her and explained the situation. "It sounded like a WI," she replied.

But such occasions have not occurred very often. We enjoyed it all but Lilian and I were a little tired at the end for we had used up a good deal of nervous energy. Though I can 'peg on' longer than many people my store of nervous energy is limited. It is this that I have to conserve. But we are all different. Some people can cook a marvellous meal while carrying on a conversation. If I try to do this, salt goes into the pudding and sugar into the potatoes so I have long ago given up the attempt.

For this reason my place may lack the light-hearted atmosphere that the amateur café-owner feels she would want to inject into her place. My excuse is that not having worn myself out too much I am, after nearly thirty years, still doing the job. I also try to save my nervous energy for my customers. Occasional customers have found, I know, that my nervous energy, or what they would prefer to call my reasonableness and good temper, is a trifle limited.

One busy afternoon, for example, I served a very enthusiastic lady outside. She thought she had never seen such a lovely district as ours and became quite friendly while praising it. She and her husband had the afternoon tea, but when she came to pay I was not at hand and I discovered that he had paid for the tea and cakes only, the usual enquiry about bread and butter not having been made. Suddenly I was furious and ran out and followed them up the road. I pointed out that nowhere would you get an afternoon tea for one and nine pence and suggested that he might have realised it. He was only casually apologetic and having no change he suggested he should pay another day. Many times have I let people do this and many times have I received postal orders from customers who find they have gone out without paying, but that was not my mood that day and he had to come back for the change. Of course, they did not come back again and three days later I received an angry letter card from the lady upbraiding me for my discourtesy. She finished by saying that she would not now be buying the many things from me that she had intended to buy. As they had sat outside and she had not even looked round the house I was doubtful about the truth of the final barb. But all the same I was very sorry about the affair. I immediately worked out the most convenient time to ring her up at her hotel to apologise. The letter, however, bore neither signature not address. I may often have been less than polite but up to now, I have never written an anonymous letter. Immediately I felt better and blamed the episode on the longsuffering members, my feet.

Yet in the passage of years how unimportant such little incidents seem. For there is always so much to take one's attention and hold it for a time until the next amusing or slightly annoying episode washes it from one's consciousness.

With such a constant stream of new helpers my 'gramophone record' of instructions and advice seems to be ground out every few months to deaf or to responsive ears. Meanwhile, thousands of customers are, as the educationists put it, 'passing through our hands'. Rarely does a week go by without a visit from a friend or relatives with news of them and acquaintances pop up nearly every day.

Customers take coffee in the sun in front of the house and compare the view with that over Lago Maggiore; families sit as long as they dare on pouring wet mornings trying to miss the eye of the waitress and of others hoping soon to take their place; small children are told to keep their hands off the wall and to drink up their milk. Infirm elderly ladies find the one high chair we keep for them and others, less infirm, find the spindle back ones in the little room rather lower than they expect. Long lost friends spin out tea at the window table and lovers drink coffee outside in the half dark of mild summer evenings. There are, too, the days when a young family troops in bearing an iced cake and candles to surprise the café in the middle of tea with a treble rendering of Happy Birthday. In June collections of ten or twelve, mostly tiny children, baulked by the weather of their expected time on the beach, are squashed together on the square table and clamour, cry and chatter their way through afternoon tea, confident that there will later be a chocolate cake or for the tiny tinies at least half.

Each autumn I review the year's working to see how methods and systems can be improved or little annoyances reduced. A quicker method may be found for a biscuit or a more accessible place for stores. Yet what I dare not change is the food I offer. What is the use when orders take the form of "You still make that lovely bread, do you? That's what we would like." Or it may be "Just some of your nice biscuits, the nutty ones, you know. The children have been looking forward to them since last summer." The fact that people on holiday do not have time to grow tired of your culinary repertoire certainly makes things easier.

Years ago the young things were all buying postcards and prints by Peter Scott; more recently everyone has collected Redouté roses. A few years ago the first cards in Chinese style were welcomed, yet some customers continue to ask for old favourites to send to their grandchildren, the same cards in fact that the children's mothers received in their childhood.

And all the time they are admiring the flowers, on quiet mornings asking if they may photograph them, or occasionally buying my watercolours of them. They photograph the garden too, and come downstairs saying that the best view of it is from the bathroom window. Some would like to buy the furniture or the matting from under our feet, or ask where we bought the tiny extra doormat.

Grasses – a painting by Mary Howe

Chapter III

Catering and Recipes

"Make a good tea now" North Country welcome

By the beginning of 1940 I had worked out a catering plan which I have adhered to with very little alteration ever since.

A man's idea of teatime heaven is toast, a woman's is scones. While it is possible to tell a man that you do not make toast, to attempt to tell a woman that there are no scones is to invite her to look at you with a mixture of scorn and incredulity, till you feel you are a disgrace to your calling. That is, of course, if it is a scone day; if it is not, nothing will make it so. There may be rows of lovely scones sitting in the kitchen saying "We shan't look as nice as this tomorrow," but today is a tea-and-cake or a pot-of-tea day, as everyone knows. All except the poor cook and she does not even know how she ought to have known.

So, rather than be worn out by 'scone anxiety', I early decided to offer a choice of an inclusive afternoon tea or tea and cakes. For, let us face it, scones are not scones the second day – their freshness is their very essence. So you have to guess each day what the weather will do which gives an indication of the sort of tea you will be serving. On wet days, by and large, people come to shelter; on fine days they come to eat. Moreover, the more scones you make, the more you have left over on a freak day, which may occur even in the season.

To serve eighty people with a tea of scones would necessitate rubbing more than a pound and a half of fat into upwards of five pounds of flour and you would be watching a hot oven for nearly an hour. People do it, but I did not choose to. Instead I took over the system we had used in Anglesey. I served scones as part of a varied afternoon tea, thus reducing the numbers needed by more than half.

Customers cannot understand it of course. They do not think that I make scones; they imagine that some fairy comes to do the job. When, however, I tell them that I make all the bread they are amazed and think how wonderful I am. But the bread is comparatively easy; it is the Irish *farle*, made without yeast. In Anglesey we kneaded it, making it into a large round which was cut into four triangles. I have cut out the kneading and I make the quantity into two long loaves which are baked on a flat sheet. In this way we reduce the quantity of crust.

From a 'big mix' of eight pounds of flour, kept in a tin, each loaf needs only three cupfuls. In about two minutes measured water blended with this makes a loaf. I use a special tool which is like a cross between a spoon and a palette knife. The fact that this tool, invaluable also for cleaning the sides of a cake-mixing bowl and gradually 'going out of production', suggests that few women besides me have discovered its usefulness.

I use this big mix also for scones, the idea being given to me by the cake-maker in Anglesey who learnt it in a subsequent job. It means that I can rub in a batch when I have some free time so that it is ready when needed. And it may be needed at short notice. On many afternoons early and late in the season when numbers fluctuate most I decide that more scones will be needed. I am seriously in the way while making them but at least no 'weighing out' and 'rubbing in' is involved. Nor, indeed, is rolling, for, working on the advice of a friend who once helped me, I now put the mixture straight into a shallow tin, smoothing it with a knife and our invaluable 'trowel'. It is cut up later when cool.

The flour for the bread matters a good deal. To give the nutty taste for which people come miles, it must be stone-ground and should be mixed with more than its own weight of white. I made some bread once using ordinary brown flour and was disappointed. A miller later explained the reason. Some grinders, being so rough, produce heat through friction, and this partly roasts the meal so imparting the nutty flavour. This bread keeps in really good condition for three days and so reduces enormously the anxiety that fluctuating numbers can cause. People sometimes ask how we cope with these fluctuations. It is done by not serving food which has to be eaten immediately, and I never serve anything stale.

This bread was to do me a good turn when the war came. The fact that I made it put me into a reserved occupation. No questions were asked about quantity and I was allowed to carry on the café. I was allowed no help except my aunt's housekeeper who, provided she worked at the hospital in the morning, was free to help me in the afternoon.

A house at the top of the hill that my married sister who lived in India, had rented for a home base, came in well for my aunt. Each winter we swapped homes with me going up to the windy heights. The doors, carefully stored in the farmer's shed, were put back and my house made a cosy retreat for her small household. We used to change over our favourite bits of furniture in autumn and again in the spring, the odd fireside chair, bookcase and folding table and things for which there was not room in the café in the summer. One year petrol rationing threatened to make this impossible, until Mr Jones' horse and cart came to the rescue. It was one of the last jobs the old carthorse undertook.

And, talking of horses, we only reminded ourselves the other day that when we first started, our milk was delivered by a horse and float twice a day. When, to save manpower, the second delivery had to be stopped we thought the world was coming to an end.

To return to teatime; the other item in the 'set tea' beside scones, bread and cake is a fruit loaf made with a little malt, syrup and chopped walnuts. It is also quick to make and keeps for three or four days. The jam is an Anglesey recipe too, but it is one that has undergone many changes over the years. The original 'glory jam' was made from rhubarb, sweet oranges, sultanas and stem ginger. People carefully picked out the sultanas and bits of ginger so now I leave them out. They also pick out the pieces of chocolate from a Maryland cake I make unless I warn them. They do not trust one far!

The jam is not quickly made as the rhubarb has to be washed and cut up though we do not peel it. The peel of the oranges was at first carefully sliced. The next step towards labour saving, and also to avoid its being picked out by those who only eat jelly marmalade, was to put it through the mincer. The recipe we now follow uses, instead of oranges, the tinned variety put up for marmalade-making. I often made the jam in the early summer, coming in from the garden about eight o'clock in the evening. It is a scramble to get it on and a light meal made and eaten before the jam needs too much attention. This is probably why it is occasionally under-boiled and fails to keep. It is not, however, often required to do so. We forgot a small dish of it once with the result that it tasted slightly 'winey'. However, I served it and said nothing. It soon came back so we apologetically served some fresh. To the next people I took the same dish saying as I served it, "The jam is a little winey. If you don't care for it we will bring you some more." "Oh, we like it like that," was the reply. So 'waste not want not' won again.

The reason I stick to glory jam apart from the fact that most people like it and find it unusual and therefore exciting, is that soft fruit has to travel so far that it is always expensive. Strawberries seldom appear for less than half-a-crown a pound and rarely in the quantities I should need. Also, by the time they are to be had, I am too busy with the café to spare time for jam-making. Rhubarb coming early can be dealt with in the slack season. The preparation of it is also a useful 'filling-in' job for the washer-up when there are few pots to deal with.

This sort of 'dove-tailing' – as one of my young helpers reminded me I called every job that 'fitted in' – is essential for the running of a seasonal business. Even the craft-shop side has its use in the scheme of things. A small café alone could hardly be made to pay, even with a fairly long season, when rates for a whole year have to be taken into account. Moreover you cannot expect to find efficient help if you offer employment for only eight or ten really busy weeks of the summer. The applicant will simply go elsewhere, so ways have to be found for filling in the quiet weeks at each end. For the café helper unpacking, marking and putting away the stock before the season begins is one of these, just as jam-making has to employ your kitchen assistant.

We never seem to manage with less than 180 lbs. of jam which means about seven boilings. Most people like it and ask for it specially, but we have the odd ones whose children have only seen red jam and mistrust any other colour. Some people think it is chutney and others are sure it is made with greengages. And red jam to many also means a 'Devonshire' tea with its attendant cream. This I am asked for from time to time by the tourist who has not really taken in Wales and its characteristics. For he is not in a lush country where everything is king-size including the sheep. Our mountain sheep give the sweetest meat you can find anywhere, but mountains do not produce strawberries or cream, at least not in our damp western climate.

So the tourist must put up with a Welsh tea. It is not, of course, a Welsh tea at all, though some local people say that the bread tastes a little like the Welsh barley bread which is still made occasionally. The fruit bread has to pose as *bara brith*, a rich fruit loaf made with yeast, and we do not attempt the Welsh pancakes which are made on a griddle.

When I first arrived I was told that ginger cake was a favourite with the Welsh and it has proved to be so with other people too. Ginger seems to be a Celtic weakness for a fondness for it spreads into Yorkshire too. I use a good quality pale-coloured ground ginger, which I used to get from the Society of Herbalists; now I have found another brand which serves. Dark-coloured ginger often tastes peppery and raw. With plenty of syrup, a little ginger-marmalade – an idea that a helper gave me – a few sultanas and chopped walnuts it makes a cake that keeps and is in fact best on the second and third day. It supplies the often-expressed need for something plain. Many people have in fact been so put off cakes by the synthetic and highly coloured confections they are offered, that one has to persuade them to try cakes at all, by assuring that they are really plain. And yet they must not look too plain. Though many people may not really care for nuts we found that, unless we put a little preserve on the ginger cake and a sprinkling of chopped nuts, it was left severely alone. People thought it looked uninteresting. The same thing applies to the fruit cake that I make occasionally. The roasted almond half-embedded in the top crust to me makes a cake. Others think it looks dull without the nut, but treat it as mere garnish and leave it on their plate.

Another popular slab cake was a copy of a wonderful confection I had eaten in Kashmir. There ground and chopped nuts make a succulent base for small pieces of chocolate. Instead of ground nuts I use up biscuit crumbs and occasionally add very finely chopped candied peel. But candied peel, along with nutmeg and caraway seeds, is an ingredient about which people have very strong tastes and feelings. For café baking they are best avoided, however much one may like them oneself.

During the rationing time my aunt provided me with chocolate and my own ration helped out, as I do not usually eat many sweets. A friend helping me liked to have a piece occasionally, as it was her favourite. She was aghast to find later on that my sweet ration was going into it. As hers was going to nieces she could not help me much, but for this item in our menu I was never really in difficulty.

In those early years I was anxious to make a 'sticky' chocolate cake. Cocoa added to cake mixture tends to make it dry out and what I wanted was a cake that was spongy and yet moist. The Anglesey recipe did not fill the bill so I experimented for a long time. I was using an ordinary Victoria sponge mixture and adding water to make up for the cocoa but time after time the cake rose and then subsided. Many tears did I shed over it and we had chocolate pudding till we were tired of it. I was being very unscientific over the affair and should have experimented along other lines. However one happy Sunday we had tea with friends and were offered a sticky chocolate cake. The recipe, a Ministry of Food one, had been in the paper but I, too occupied with my own line of experiment, had not read it. For some odd reason black treacle is used, but when this was replaced with syrup I found that the recipe made the cake I had been hoping for. I still make this, not in two or three large cakes to a one pound of flour batch, but in six smaller ones. Made so, they spend less time in the oven, so are subject to fewer hazards of temperature fluctuation. They also have less tendency to be over-cooked on the outside. And, almost more important, the portions cut from them present a smaller drying surface than does a thin slice from a large deep cake.

In the war years it had to be served plain, but now, with four processes lavished on its finishing it is the star turn of the café; the only cake that really looks professional. It seems, however, that many people who come to us for tea do not particularly want a professional-looking cake. They enjoy something different for a change. All the world but I can make a light sponge cake and dress it with icing, butter filling or lemon cheese, so why should I join the competition? It is probably because I produce cakes and bread that are quickly made that I can keep my prices down.

The world is divided between those who look upon cookery as an art and those who would like to turn it into a sort of science. To my mind the baking branch is something of a hybrid between the two.

Good cake-makers include the hit-and-miss variety whose products always do, in fact, turn out a success. These people can never give away a recipe for they have none. They use no weights but do everything in true artistic style by 'guessing', as they make a point of altering the recipe just slightly every time, in a way which they can never quite recall. Perhaps they do not wish to.

On the other side of the scale are those who will trust only a recipe, never themselves. In one detail at least their trust is often sadly misplaced and the reason is a scientific one. For how many recipes finish with the words, 'Add a little milk or milk and water to make a dropping consistency'? This would be fine if the word *little* were qualified and the make of flour stipulated. A given amount of liquid used with a strong flour will produce a mixture which will pour into the tins; use it with a weak flour and your result will be as the books say.

Some self-raising flours come into each category, though most plain flours tend to be weak. So it is wise to find the kind that you like and stick to it. Keep also to a liquid measure and ignore all temptations to add or withhold, bearing in mind that the temperature of your kitchen and your utensils can vary considerably and so affect the appearance of the mixture.

One variable, however, you could consider when making your ginger cake or chocolate slab is the size of the eggs. Large eggs will make a mixture appear soft. Yet when cooked, the egg goes solid. So the larger the eggs the more milk can be added. You will find that, up to a point, the more liquid your mixture can be persuaded to take the more moist your cake will be. It is for the baker to find the point and then stick to what will, in the end, be her own, not the book's, recipe.

Some people I know do not care for the cakes we serve, but for them there is the 'plain tea'. We do try to be accommodating and for those who do not care for cakes we offer the first part of the set tea only. People often argue with me about my prices. They say I do not charge enough. Perhaps my motto about waste enables me to keep my charges reasonable for I try to avoid waste of effort as well as of material. The public tends to forget that it is often not the food that is costly but the service. Yet many people who live in Wales will make a round trip of fifty miles to have tea and because they do not like the idea of bread and butter, refuse the afternoon tea and order tea and cakes only. There is nearly as much washing up involved for their seven shilling order as for a ten shilling one. And after all they do not need to eat everything in the set tea.

Some people even ask for 'as little as possible'. To one man who gave this order I said, "And would you go into the Ritz and order a boiled egg?." I had, of course, chosen my man carefully and we all laughed and he explained that the hotel was feeding them too well. All of which I know, and that is why my prices must be kept down. For many people are paying heavily enough for their holiday without having costly extras as well. This does not, however, apply to those who have taken a run out from home. If they were visiting many cafés that I know in Derbyshire and Yorkshire they would have to pay twice what I ask, and have no option. But I am not complaining because I know perfectly well that there are many, many occasions when we run short of food and are only too grateful to the people who order just tea and cakes.

I have often spent a good deal of ingenuity in trying to persuade customers to order what I want them to have. We try all sorts of formulae. Some people shy off an 'afternoon tea' thinking it will turn out to be a huge Yorkshire spread. So for them we vary the name and call it 'the small set tea'. The word home-made usually does the trick, though on the other hand we get people who only want cream cakes and 'fancies'. To them we take the chocolate cake hoping it will get by.

I have never yet had a customer who asked what I would best like to get rid of; that would be expecting too much! The nearest to such consideration came one dim afternoon. We had been quite busy and at about five o'clock people came who were in a furnished flat close by. The wife explained that she had said to her husband, "There they are at the Bobbing Boats, they will have done lots of baking and no one will come to eat it, we must go and help them out." I was very grateful for the thought and even more for the luck which ordained that I had just about enough left to serve them.

We can sometimes tell what an order will be from the accent in which it is delivered. The local Welsh people nearly always come early and do themselves well with afternoon tea. For they are not inordinately proud of their own cooking and are ready to try someone else's! Not so the Scots. I say they trust no one's cooking but their own. They ask for 'a pot of tea just', or perhaps some cakes which they do not really expect to enjoy. In this way they are often, after a few visits, converted to the full tea and are high in praise of it, even of the shortbreads!

People from the far south do not eat tea; they only drink it, which is not surprising when you consider how few teatime dainties have emanated from south of the Thames. Maids of honour make a poor showing against Bakewell tart, Eccles cake, Chorley cake, Goosnargh cake, Grasmere gingerbread, parkin, scones and *bara brith*.

One gentleman from those parts, however, came one day about five-fifteen in the afternoon and was hungry. At least he asked for a 'lyte' tea. I could not decide whether it was a late tea he wanted or a light one, but reckoning that our afternoon tea, served as it would be in about five minutes' time, qualified for both descriptions I took it to him. He seemed quite satisfied.

When I first started I made what one of our customers appreciatively called 'currant pasty'. The adjective was pronounced rather like the word the French use for their non-existent hot water[2]. So I knew where he came from and that he knew what was what in the cake line. There was always a piece of currant pasty for him for many years and he was always known as 'currant pasty' in the kitchen. We

---

[2] Margaret Irwin says in her book, '*That Great Lucifer*', that footnotes should only be used for original research. Perhaps the following story about French plumbing would qualify. In a hotel in Savoy I found that hot water came from the cold tap and cold only out of the hot. Pleased to air my French I told the *patron*. "Ah," he replied, "the plumber made a mistake." But he did not look pleased. "Bother the English," his expression said. "They would discover my plan for saving my precious hot water. Other nationalities would have assumed that the boiler had gone out and said nothing."

had at home always called this cake 'Flat Annie'. The currantless part at each end of the oblong could not be served, but it made a delicious tart with fruit and cream and was known as 'Annie's End'.

In spite of much practice, however, my pastry-rolling never improved. Intended to be an oblong of about fourteen inches by eleven it usually turned out like a map of England. It was good pastry though, short, but not too short for it had to cut neatly; in fact it was a little flaky. The secret was that I mixed it with warm, or in cold weather, hot water. I make it no longer for it took too much time, hence my willingness to hand on the trick.

For I do not give my recipes away. I am always rather surprised that people should expect it, yet some do. If you are in business they are after all part of your stock-in-trade that you have probably taken some time to perfect. I always feel that if people really want a recipe they can find something near to it in a book and alter or adapt it themselves.

The idea for one cake I make was supplied by a visit to a pleasant café in Suffolk. There a shallow Victoria sponge was topped with chocolate icing and sprinkled with browned almonds. Never having had much luck with Victoria sponge, I use my ginger cake recipe leaving out the nuts and fruit. The ginger flavour blends pleasantly with the chocolate though many people remove the lovely browned almond I put on each piece. The recipe for the icing can be given away. It is simply a bar of plain chocolate put into a double pan, or a bowl standing in a pan. To avoid lumps forming do not break into pieces, but melt it as it is with a cube of lard. Pour on while still warm and spread with a dry knife. If the tins are already lined three slab cakes to cut into about sixty portions can be made in less than half-an-hour. This preparation and cleaning can be reduced to a minimum by using the new, but rather expensive, non-stick cake tins. For the hard wear that they receive in a café they are definitely worth the money.

The half-hour in which cakes are made is not, as some of my customers imagine, the one going up to seven in the morning, for I have never been an early riser. My excuse is that I am expected to be still cheerful by teatime and a long morning might make this difficult. The truth is that I come to life at night.

I used to try rushing all the baking in during the morning. Then I found that I had to be about in the evening when, with students enjoying the coffee-serving, I was left with not quite enough to do. Now I spread the work out and have time to spare for people in the morning, using part of the evening to prepare for a batch of baking. After ten o'clock, the café empty and the lights out, I can get down to things and quite enjoy it. Preparation for the next day can be done while the cakes are in the oven or better still there is time to walk along the water front.

The waves are lapping quietly in the little bay or lapping against the sea wall; the air is deliciously soft and fresh after the sickly-smelling kitchen and I can relax knowing that another day has been happily worked through. If there have been difficulties the size of the starlit sky helps to put them into proportion. Sometimes I have a chat with other busy villagers who are taking the air before turning in, or I may go to the little jetty for a paddle or if the tide is high have a swim from the steps.

On other evenings I may have a leisurely drink in the darkening garden where that most fragrant rose Mme. Alfred Carrière still shows blush white against the stone wall and there is the smell of the jasmine that grows near the apple tree. For it is no use trying to divide busy August days into work and leisure. Almost the whole of the fourteen hours is work, but, spread out and taken slowly, much of it can be savoured and tiredness thereby reduced.

I find it is sometimes better to stay up a little later and be sure of sleeping well. In the morning I am not down much before eight o'clock. When I am on my own three jobs compete for the first half-hour: baking, 'hoovering' the mattings, or dealing with that dust and dirt collector the front doorstep. They are not done in the same order every day, but they help to wake me up and give me an appetite for breakfast. By the time I am ready for it the post has arrived and I can digest that too. By this time the children are passing on their way to school and if the weather is cool or dull I like to watch them. In early summer the bottom of the garden is by this time in sun and I can carry my breakfast tray there. A late breakfast also splits up the morning making elevenses unnecessary, or a drink of Ribena enough.

A scramble of jobs follows breakfast: letters, baking, a stint of dusting, table-polishing, coffee-making, window-cleaning, an endless list. For the tables once a week I use an electric drill which has a polishing head attached. It is noisy and not very easy to use as too much pressure can take the polish off instead of putting a mirror surface on, so partly for safety and in their own interest I do not ask the students to use it. The sheen, however, is lasting and saves me much rubbing.

Soon after ten o'clock I issue forth with a teapot of water, some fresh flowers to fill the gaps, tray, scissors and duster. I find that if I do the flowers about this time I have a chance to talk to early customers who are often themselves keen flower-arrangers. By these means I am also able to convey an impression of leisureliness which the state of the kitchen would hardly really bear out.

We are not, of course, untidy; in a small place you just cannot be, and we believe in putting as good a face on things as possible. People often remark on the calm atmosphere which prevails when they feel sure that all is not calm behind the scenes.

This idea of doing a little acting was first put into my mind when I worked in a settlement in the East End. We youngsters were given the job of preparing for a conference and spent most of the morning hauling chairs about the grimy passages of a row of old houses which formed the Princess Club. I was also given the job of doing the flowers for the speaker's table and finding a suitable picture to hang behind it. I found a landscape with a hint of yellow in the sky which was picked up by the vase of yellow roses which had come in that morning from Kent. It was my first attempt at making a flower arrangement into a whole. Then at two o' clock the warden told us to disappear and come back in half-an-hour 'looking as though we had never done a hand's turn of work in our lives'. How well I have remembered her wise words. There is a useful saying about being poor without seeming poor. That warden was trying to show us that the word 'poor' could on occasion usefully be replaced by the word 'busy'.

Early and late in the season I can be really leisurely, have an early breakfast and walk into town for shopping, calling on the way back to see a friend. As I shall be making jam late at night or perhaps decorating, I feel justified in enjoying my little outing. Indeed that is the fun of being your own boss, you can, within limits, arrange your work to suit yourself.

The customers fortunately set the limits, and to see them sitting on the garden seat when you get back makes it all feel worthwhile. They act too as a stimulus if you feel tired and if you merely feel lazy, and you find the jobs getting done because they simply have to be done. In fact the most tiring day is often the quiet one. On the busy one you are spurred on to move more than you could have imagined possible and you feel refreshed rather than tired at the end of it all.

Serving coffee keeps me going for the morning. I still make it in the old-fashioned way using brown jugs and taking two brews from each lot of coffee rather than one weak one. I really should change and use one of the modern percolators, but I am not sure the coffee would be so well liked, and the compliments mean much. Also, good coffee brings more customers.

A good deal is talked about the secret of making coffee. If you start with really good material it is difficult to spoil it whether you pour on boiling water or mix it with cold and bring it to the boil. It should, however, never touch aluminium both for your health's sake and for the sake of the flavour. I use an enamel pan for boiling it up from cold. The reason for the brown jug is the same as for the brown teapot. It is just a matter of physics. A dark-coloured object absorbs heat more readily than a light one, so the pot you have heated ready for your tea or coffee is really hot. A white one would need much more heating and you probably would not have the patience to leave it long enough or pour enough boiling water into it to soak it thoroughly.

We keep the coffee hot for serving in an iron cauldron which I bought from a ship's chandler when I first arrived in Wales. Before coming to me it had probably sailed the Seven Seas and made delicious *lobscouse* for generations of sailors. The old chandler has gone long ago. He also sold slender tallow candles made in the town. If anything happened to my cauldron I should feel lost.

Well lagged and about a quarter full of boiling water it sits on a gas ring and keeps hot two jugs of black coffee, one of milk and one of

63

mixed coffee. To serve large numbers it has to be kept filled up as its contents are used and when we are very busy more supplies have to be heated in non-stick and stainless steel pans. So it takes a little watching on a busy morning, but when a constant stream of coffee is needed for more than two hours it does the job very well. Moreover it does it without the hissing and steam-making associated with 'instant' equipment. I doubt if I could, in any case, find room for the equipment one sees in a cafeteria, because in the afternoon the cauldron is covered with a board and trays of tea are set on it.

The cream is always taken off the milk first because it merely wastes itself in skin if left to stand hot. I like it in tea – though I know it is not everyone's taste – so it is put aside to fortify our already rich whole milk for the afternoon. I sometimes wonder if the compliments that my tea earns from those who, like myself, find it quite a different drink served with creamy milk.

Two girls who helped me and afterwards started a café in Derbyshire had a daunting experience on their opening day. Their friends were all invited and everyone had put off coming till nearly eleven o'clock to be sure of seeing everyone else. The coffee had been made early, good and strong and mixed with hot milk to be all ready to pour. When the customers arrived and the coffee was poured it curdled. They could not understand it but it had happened to me – most things have – and when I went to see them the next winter I was able to give them the reason. The coffee was very fresh and was too acid for the overheated milk. Adding a little cold water would have put it right. In their case they had to start again, but luckily the café is over a dairy so more milk was near at hand.

I close for an hour from about one o'clock till two, sometimes for a little more. If at all possible, in the quieter part of the year, I have something with salad in the garden. Then, remembering Churchill's dictum that a change is as good as a rest, I do a job in the garden, tie up a rose or stake some of the Michaelmas daisies.

Some people wonder why I bother about a midday meal, especially when they want me to make one for them instead. They assume that it would be wiser to carry on with a snack at midday and have a meal when I finish. I should, however, be too tired then to enjoy it, and in any case I prefer a high tea in the evening. When I first started we did, of course, serve a light lunch occasionally for we had to catch at any straw of custom that came our way. I remember on one occasion not eating our own lunch till twenty to three. But in those days we served very few teas.

By employing extra people in the middle of the day we could serve lunches and on some days we might do quite well. We are, however, rather too remote to have a regular *clientele* and I am afraid the quiet days would cancel out the busy ones, as well as adding considerably to my worries. It is wise I think to make up your mind at the beginning what you are going to do or what you are best 'cut out' to do. Then, with slight variations, you should stick to your original plan and be satisfied.

Only two people have ever offered to take my place over if I wished to sell it, and both have said they would make it into a restaurant. I do not think they realised what a very short and rushed season they would have.

If they found the kitchen rather inadequate they would, however, find it tolerably cool. We are indeed lucky for the jutting-out larder prevents even the June sun from reaching us. In close damp weather, particularly at midday when the dinner is being cooked and the scones are in the oven it can, however, get very hot. We used to find that the rain drifted in through the window, but a glass-topped open porch at the back has taken care of that. The window in the back door can also be opened to give ventilation in the larder and, if necessary, the door can be made to keep open, as a simple stay has been let into one of the tiles of the floor.

It is small and inexpensive details such as these that make for easy working. And even when some day the place becomes once more a private house they will still add to its comfort.

Pelargoniums – a painting by Mary Howe

Chapter IV

Stock and Customers

The customer is always right. Traditional

I do not pretend to be a *clever* business woman, at least not in the usually accepted meaning of that term. I believe that the retail trade should be looked upon as the means of supplying as wide an assortment of people as possible with what they are looking for. The smart and fashion-conscious must be catered for as well as those who do not really know what they want and there are enough shops to do it for them. But the minority also have a claim to consideration. And at least a few shopkeepers in the kingdom can make a modest living and have an interesting job trying to satisfy such people's perfectly legitimate needs.

To be one of these not very vocal people and to go into many of the large stores is to come out, often empty-handed, with the feeling that there is something seriously wrong with one. If anyone is to blame, it is not just the new type of *vendeuse* who is said to be unable to care less. Rather are the old and entrenched buyers responsible. It is, however, their system and their taste and ideas which keep the little shops ticking over. So we should not complain, but go with our requirements to them.

How often am I told by customers that they have hunted high and low for the thing which they have triumphantly bought from me! I have also frequently been told that my stock is 'better' than that of a famous shop in the Tottenham Court Road. I take this praise with a pinch of salt for I know that shop well. Did these people but know it, it has provided me with many of my ideas. For not only do they show interesting craft work there but they often display the maker's name by it. Discreet enquiries with the head saleswoman or with people from the Crafts Centre or the Rural Industries Bureau furnishes one with their address.

Probably those who praise my shop were feeling tired and footsore when they were in London on holiday. Relaxed and having consumed a good tea or a stimulating cup of coffee in my shop, they are feeling very different. To what extent the catering helps the sales I have no means of finding out, but in the rather isolated place in which I have put up my sign, I am sure the assistance is considerable.

Another factor which helps the shopkeeper in a holiday district is the fact that husbands and wives can look round in relative peace and quiet instead of fighting off the Saturday morning crowds in their own High Street.

I make a point of never telling an enquirer there is 'no demand' for what she happens to be enquiring about. For there obviously is one as she is demanding it. If I do not stock it, it may be something that I have no intention of stocking. For it is no use trying to mix 'rubbish' with other stock. The rubbish spoils the rest. Otherwise I tell her where I think she may be successful, or, if it is a thing that I would like to sell, I admit quite frankly that I have not yet been successful in running it to ground.

Several customers have helped me find new pottery by telling me of craftsmen in their district. But I make no claims to be exclusive or highbrow and I sell quantities of ephemeral costume jewellery as well as good craft work. But, though I know I make frequent mistakes in selecting jewellery, I do try to find pieces that either look good, have style or fill what I imagine to be a real gap. Into the last category fall, for example, beads, ear-rings and brooches in navy blue and I rarely have enough of them.

I attribute mistakes that I make partly to the same feelings that have overcome many visitors to the shop in the Tottenham Court Road [Heal's]. For I am sometimes feeling not only tired when I am choosing stock at the Fair but I have also seen more than enough. A visit to a trade fair, though an exciting and stimulating experience, can also be a very tiring one. There is so much to walk past that one does not want, as well a bewildering variety of what one does. Also, the one I go to in February seems undecided whether to freeze you or boil you like a lobster, so it is difficult to know what to wear. You know pretty well where you will be very hot, but on the same day you may find yourself very cold. In neither situation is my brain at its best, particularly as in some parts of the Fair there is a woeful shortage of chairs. So, if I make mistakes I have a useful barrage of excuses.

Many of the firms are only too willing to make things easier by sending their representatives to call on me. And there is no doubt that it is really wiser to choose what suits one's shop when seen *in situ*, rather than under the gaudy lights of a trade fair. For several reasons I discourage these visits, partly because the journeys are timed too early in the year and my place is not yet open. Or if I see the traveller later, the goods also arrive later, at a time when we are too busy to unpack, check them and mark them. Also a representative's call so often coincides with a tea or coffee rush and I do not like to waste his time or ask him to come again. The chief reason, however, for ordering early is that imported goods, such as a good deal of the jewellery, are on quota and the most attractive lines often sell out quite early in the spring.

With books, one of my most successful ventures, the situation is different. The travellers have a pretty good idea of the sort of thing I stock and are quite willing to bring their briefcase into the kitchen. There while I make biscuits or serve coffee we go through the lists together, and the books appear, ready marked, a few days later. I have had great interest from selling books, and children's books for all ages are splendid at the moment. Grannies buy them for they do not like hunting through the crowded shops; parents buy them, sheaves of them, because they cannot find what they want at home; and children buy them because some are just what they want for Auntie's half-crown which has been burning a hole in their pocket all day.

I also sell a surprising number of paper-backs and they are not all novels. Books on slightly esoteric subjects fill their finders with delight, though they may stay on my shelves for longer than I like. But others on architecture, mathematics, old silver and furniture, art and history never sit there long. As a result of this I have myself become an even more confirmed 'dipper'. I have also been introduced to writers whom I would not otherwise have tried.

Books on watching wildlife are not bought for children only. We have a steady sale of bird books, books on Snowdonia, on the sea coast as well as illustrated floras and identification books about the varied life of the seashore. People on holiday do not want to be met in the bookshop with, "No we haven't it in stock, but we can get it for you." They want to take it away with them to use there and then, so I always have a stock of these books to hand, as well as garden, flower arranging, cookery books and books on wine and wine-making.

The imported goods are attractive to some customers more on account of the strangeness of their place of origin, perhaps, than for their intrinsic interest. For we all like to romanticise one another, and many people trying to drape at least an aura of romance around me, decide that I 'winter abroad'. And from far-flung corners of the continent of Europe they imagine that I return with cases of exciting goods to sell. I hate to disillusion them and do it as gently as I can; but I have to tell them about the trade fair I go to where, no exotic travellers, but mere commercial agents collect goods from all over the world.

I have come to the conclusion that many people, apart from their visits to my café to obtain a good tea for the family, never look in a craft shop window. One can tell this from little remarks they let fall. And they often buy a brooch or a pot in such a way that it is quite obvious that they are only buying it to support me. I bless them for it. I realise it is their kind way of ensuring that I shall still be there for tea next time they come to Wales. Perhaps it is another way of saying what many customers say when their holiday is over, "Goodbye; look after yourself." They might almost as well say, "We shall want coffee next year, too, you know."

There are other people who display their ignorance of the ordinary things around them in a rather less disarming way. Many customers are convinced that we make all the pottery ourselves, though some of it is obviously factory-made. Recently when I served a lady, using with pride our now fine grey tea china, she said, "Is this yours?" I knew what she meant, but I felt that I must explain that fine bone china like that is not made in small hand potteries. Others ask if the tea china is made in Wales. Presumably they think that Swansea and Nantgarw are still in production, or do they think at all?

Unfortunately the oddments of pottery that I do buy on holiday abroad – for I can never resist a pottery shop – are usually put into use for ash trays or jam dishes and being rather precious to me they are strictly 'not for sale'. Some of them would give interesting ideas to potters in this country, but potters are conservative folk. Rightly so in many instances, for what could be more satisfying than the lovely slipware jugs and casseroles turned out in the Cotswolds and Devon. But some potters complain and say that people will not buy handmade pots and give a craftsman a decent living. And this is often because he insists on making the same shaped things and he will tell you, believe it or not, the reason is that he happens to *like* making *just* those pots. They are not all, it is true, quite so independent, but many of them are.

Butter dishes are a case in point. Most people's idea of them is something with a lid. A local pottery used to make a pleasant one like this. Then they costed it out and found that, with all the processes involved and the extra space required in the kiln, it was not economic. I can well believe it. But must a butter dish have a lid? Is it not more important that it should have a handle as traditional potters give it in Spain and France? This makes it so much easier to pick up. And presumably if it is to be used more than once without refilling it will be kept in a cupboard, so why the lid?

Beside a practical butter dish, flat oblong dishes are another item that the housewife looks for, because they are so attractive for sandwiches. One source of these has completely dried up and I suspect that the reason is the high proportion of kiln loss. For these are made from slices cut from a cube of clay then beaten over a mould and left to dry. A thrown plate, being flat, has a tendency to sit down in the kiln, but a flat dish which has not been subjected to the centring and centrifugal forces which come into play in the throwing process will warp even more, unless very skilfully made. The clay and glaze must be exactly suited to kiln conditions. This is why these attractive dishes tend to be expensive.

All the more reason why I rejoice in my good fortune. For I found at a fair a south country potter so skilled that he can produce splendid specimens cheaper than I have found anywhere else. It is a 'find' like this which makes the job of buying occasionally exciting. The reverse side of the medal is that shops in his locality have discovered these pots too and go and collect what they want. So I can never get quite as much of his pottery as I would like.

How enormously pottery prices vary! People sometimes ask me the reason and I wonder if they do the same in a dress or hat shop. What diverse replies 'Modom' would receive if she tried doing that! Though perhaps they would be no more inaccurate than the reasons I try to produce. The fundamental reason is that some pots are made in a factory and some in a studio, though factory pots are often hand-thrown and some studio pots are moulded. You can sometimes see the mould marks if you look carefully.

In large stores where clothes are sold the difference of origin is rarely recognised and the mass-produced dresses are carefully segregated by being shown on different floors. In a craft shop the pots of very different origin are shown side by side. But there are also variations within each category and, in the case of studio pots, the difference in price may be due, other things being equal, to the organising power of the potter.

Other things unfortunately are not always equal. For some potters, bursting with ideas, start up in business before they are really sufficiently trained. In that case the purchaser may pay not only for verve and originality; he pays for some of the potter's mistakes, in other words for the remainder of his training. All of which gives the customer an interesting time, for he has a chance to use his judgement.

And this is why I think a craft shop should have as wide a choice as possible on offer. One way that I have achieved this in the past has been by never letting my stock get really low. Then each year I start with a fair selection and add to it,. Some of the same again being bought, but nearly always a good quantity of something different. This is all very incorrect, I know, for it means that I never have a clearance sale. Instead a table of reduced items appears in the spring and autumn. During the rest of the season we put 'reduced' tickets on things that are due to be 'moved on'. I also occasionally reduce something in this category when the customer happens to be an old and valued one.

I work it this way because I imagine that the rest of the world is like me and loves a bargain. At sale time I will go into a shop whose doors I would never darken at any other time. But I do not want people to do that in my shop! I prefer that the old and regular customers who are often the spring and autumn visitors, and people who buy a great deal from me at other times, should have the bargains.

And what about the really old stock? I find that if it has been well chosen and is really suitable for my trade, it will sell, even after many years. If it is not right for my shop, I might as well call it my charity and give it away.

One little aside about stocking a shop will perhaps surprise the layman, though it is an accepted fact to those in many kinds of trade. This is that things sell in 'runs'. If, after selling a few of a new thing, you order perhaps twice as many more, that line will die immediately. Something else will take its place and you may sell no more of your newly ordered stock for a long time if at all. There seems to be no way of accounting for this, but it happens even with goods in constant demand such as greengrocery. One day everyone wants oranges; the shop sells out and orders more than usual, when the entire world immediately goes on a diet of apples or pears.

It does also happen that you sell a few of a comparatively new thing one year and decide to make a feature of it the next; and you will be lucky. People will buy them and tell you that they have seen similar elsewhere but not as pleasant or as reasonable as yours, and you will go on selling them all through the season. You have, it would appear – as the civil servants say – found the right thing, in the right style, at the right price and you have stocked enough of them. It does not happen very often.

A wide and varied stock, especially if you are mixing crafts with catering, gives customers confidence. They know you mean business, whereas a few oddments, obviously from the same stable, give the impression that you have not chosen them but have been prevailed on by a travelling agent to 'have a go'.

And yet though plenty will often please, you need to be tactful for people love to feel that they have found something different. For example, I may display a distinguished-looking brooch which will be purchased with glee say, on Tuesday. I will be wise to ask if the lady is staying in the village for, if it is coffee time, we shall probably see

73

her again. Is it good business to put out a second identical brooch and, in hoping to sell another, to risk her seeing it? Or is it wiser as well as kinder to leave her with her illusions and husband the rest of the stock till next week? For most people have no sort of idea how much a shop sells. They will notice and admire a rug on the first day of their holiday and be amazed to find it no longer there on the last. So the exciting brooch they buy is to them the only one and they will probably tell their friends what a marvellous shop they have found. Does long-term strategy or short-term tactics pay best? I really do not know, but I prefer the strategy. And having thought all this out you will find a customer most anxious to find some beads exactly like hers for her friend. You will be lucky if you have them!

Again you may find that a certain line will go quite well and ask the agent for more. I found this with some hand-blocked note books and lampshades. They were not trail-blazers, but they sold steadily. I was, however, told with regret that the artist had stopped making then and taken a teaching job as her products did not sell. When I expressed surprise the agent replied, "But here they have you behind them." I pointed out that I am no saleswoman, but he stuck to his point and emphasised that it was because they fitted in with my place that they had sold. And he was right, of course. But it is also true that things that do fit in will sell better if you have a fair stock of these and if you exhibit them in more that one part of the shop. For example, I used to display all the wood tableware as I often see it in other shops when I go to have a look round, to buy a birthday card and at the same time to get new ideas. Yet seeing this done in other people's shops, I realise how mistaken the system is. For it gives the impression that wood is for a certain sort of person only and has no appeal for the rest. Mixed here and there with, say, stainless steel or wood-topped spice jars, it gives the customer ideas. People will look at it who otherwise might never give it a thought.

And giving people ideas is a great part of the shopkeeper's job. So many different sorts of people are looking for ideas. To start with there are, the 'cat and canary' presents to think of. Many people have a kind neighbour who has fed pussy on the back doorstep every day for a fortnight, or one equally accommodating, who has taken in the budgie. What shall they buy as a thank you? It is with such people in mind that

I choose many of the pieces of pottery and jewellery I stock. A wider assortment of these can be found by opening the drawers and cupboards. In fact I find occasionally that some of my customers know where things are stored better than I do. At one time they so enjoyed making even more chaotic the collection of shallow boxes in what was known as the jewellery drawer, that when I had a new cupboard made fitted with velvet-lined trays they were quite put out.

If presents in this category are fairly easy to find the same cannot be said of gifts for those precious home-helps. If you suggest something homely she turns out to be very smart; china is no good for she is a smasher and is only employed to do fires and the kitchen floor; aprons are evidently tactless; of jewellery she already has a plethora. But she is very good at pot plants, so good in fact that the hopeful present-giver has handed all her own to her. We then compare notes of our experience of these exasperating products of nature, cyclamen that go off and cinerarias that collapse. And for the lucky lady who can persuade them to live, we would find between us the flower pot of her dreams.

An even more difficult giftee – horrid word which I only use for a chance to deplore it – is 'Aunt Millicent who has everything'. Of anything you bring along she already has hundreds and thousands. I secretly hope that for her 'just the thing' is something I am particularly anxious to sell. It might indeed, if truth were known, turn out to be something slightly 'old stock'. So I hold my fire for a bit. Jewellery again proves to be no good for she has the 'real thing' and a silk scarf is useless for she does not go out. Notelets often solve the problem and a china beaker would be acceptable if it were not so large. It is strange that English china manufacturers do not realise how little the Aunt Millicents of the world drink for their 'nightcap'. They do not relish it in the bottom of a deep container of half-pint capacity however prettily the old-fashioned roses, with which it is decorated, blend with their sitting-room. The Germans have been more imaginative and have produced charming small cruets in porcelain. 'Just the thing for her lunch tray' especially as 'all the silver has been put away'. So we sell another of them with tiny pale blue flowers this time, or shall it be roses in fine grey outline?

From this it may appear that I spend a great deal of my time in selling. This, however, is not so for there is so often something in the kitchen requiring attention. I only come to the rescue when I am asked. Judging others by myself, I feel that people prefer to look round in peace provided that an offer has been made to lift down anything out of reach or to find other colours in anything that appeals.

People are naturally always on the look-out for presents for children. A favourite one is a mug or plate with their name or a pleasant and clear nursery rhyme decoration. One never, however, has enough of the right names and very often John fails to sell because you have not the necessary Judith to go with it, but only Judy. As the mugs are such steady sellers I keep to a 'rock bottom' price for them. They should be sold for at least five and threepence but if more than one is purchased at a time we charge only five shillings. It is amazing how many more we have sold as a result of this little selling stunt.

Up to this year good decorated 'children's ware', as it is termed in the trade, has been difficult to find. Much of that made in England whether china, often above my customers' price bracket, or the cheaper earthenware, has had poor or too small and detailed decoration. Some artist has at last, however, produced good nursery rhyme drawings in clear colours and, what has surprised me considerably, she has been able to sell them to several different firms. I had seen them first in a furniture shop where I was given the name of the maker. As this name did not appear in the fair catalogue I thought I had remembered it wrongly so sought out one that seemed similar. No sign of what I was looking for there, but my eye being caught by something at the entrance to the next room, I went in, to find behind the door the mugs and plates that I sought. Luckily this pottery produced other things that I liked also, so I was able to make a worthwhile order. I have long ago found that a great many small orders involve more paper work than I have time for. In any case firms will only accept an order above a certain value. They have their packing costs to watch too.

After this I saw the same nursery rhyme decoration in numerous collections. No doubt the pottery proprietors were as surprised as I was when they found the design they had bought reproduced by their competitors. Such matters are properly their affair and no doubt they will all sell satisfactory quantities of the ware. For my part it is disappointing because I imagined that I had found something 'different'.

I will admit that customers' desire to buy something Welsh used to meet with little encouragement from me. I preferred, as I often said, that an object should sell 'on its own merits' rather than because it happened to have been made in a certain area of the earth's surface by a craftsman possibly not indigenous.

However, I have changed my attitude on this subject. More good pottery has been produced by Welsh people and since, I must confess it, Welsh tapestries have become fashionable. I do not even now attempt to sell anything of tapestry except bags and holdalls. But, tempted by lovely coats and jerkins made in it, I have looked more carefully at Welsh wool shops and realised that many of their wares are suitable for mine. Ties are an example with excellent and fashionable colour blends, as well as wool squares, stoles, aprons and knee rugs.

I used to say that the Welsh are not craftsmen. After all, if they make some of the best teachers, preachers, lawyers, actors and singers and if they also fill the top places in the Civil Service as well as often helping to govern us as well as themselves, I feel there must be some little niche left for the English. However, I have changed my views on this matter also, and admit that they can pretty well do anything they set their mind to. Perhaps, however, they are not very good organisers and that is why they cannot run a small café and craft shop as well as certain of the English can.

But with all this the Welsh are modest. Their lack of self confidence, or rather, their plain inferiority complex endears them to the too self-assured English with their odd idea of humour. The Welsh lay no extravagant claims to a monopoly in that commodity; they display it instead in the most delightful ways. For they have, in themselves, a splendid home-made subject on which to practise it. As Berta Ruck, herself part-Welsh has said, "The keynote of the Welshman's humour is that he does not mind poking fun at himself."

In any case, craftsmen or not, foreign visitors and Americans in particular not unnaturally like to take home something that they know is made in Wales.

We do not get very many Americans as we are off the main tourist centres, and most of those who come are of Welsh extraction. I was told a story of one by a steward at the National Eisteddfod when it was held in Pwllheli. In the crafts section a woodworker was showing bread boards the edge of which he had decorated with carving based on local ear-marks [identification notches on sheep's ears]. An American was thrilled to recognise ear-marks which had been used for generations on his ancestors' farm. He ordered several to be sent out to the States as presents.

One day in the café a middle-aged lady asked me what I stocked that was Welsh. Thinking she might have in mind bulky things such as quilts, I suggested that she went to the Welsh Craft shop in the town where they had a wide selection and were used to despatching them all over the world. But she was adamant. The things she sought for her husband's brother must come from my shop. Her voice and manner proclaimed her nationality. And to anyone familiar with the many and various types of American her quiet-voiced, pale and charming husband would have been equally unmistakable. He was, I guessed, in his early sixties. He greeted me, but took no part in the discussion and, after a leisurely look round and a restful gaze at the view, he appeared to be totally immersed in the books.

When I began to collect a few Welsh things for his wife to look at, she explained the situation. Her husband's father had been born in this house, hence the interest and her desire to take something back that she had bought here. "But," I said, when she told me this, "An American gentleman, a Mr Davies, came about four years ago and told me that his father was born in this house." She was delighted when I remembered this visit. I certainly had. As a May afternoon was quietening off I had time to take in the very American physiognomy of a man who with his wife and two friends had just finished tea in the window. His chiselled, and at the same time fluid, features might have decorated the front of Time magazine. He looked round thoroughly then came down the hall to ask if he might take a photograph of this charming little house where his father had been born. It was with the very latest of cameras and after a few minutes he presented me with a black and white print. He then asked if he could see the garden and afterwards I took him and his wife to see the rest of the house and the superb view from the upstairs windows. He was charmed with it all and so pleased to see how I had altered these windows to be like the twelve-paned ones that were in the house at first. For his father would first have known it when it was only twenty or thirty years old.

He was delighted to see it all looking so pretty and being put to such good use. His father, he told me, had taken his young wife to Liverpool and three years after he himself was born, they had emigrated. So a Welsh couple had produced a child who had become the loud-voiced, extraverted enthusiastic Yankee of everyone's imagination. The Mr Davies whose wife brought him to see his father's birthplace four years later was the youngest of the family.

Most of the foreigners who come our way are students or *au pair* girls. We often remark on their informed taste in pottery. If I fear that a piece may be a little highbrow I often say to myself, "Never mind, a foreign student will probably like it."

Older foreigners are often brought by business friends with whom they are staying, people who often arouse my envy by their facility in their guests' language. I can mimic most sounds after a little practice but I have never mastered any language. The result is that I can ask a question in a pretty good accent only to be answered by a flood of language beyond my comprehension. However, my five words of three languages give me a good deal of fun.

Some old customers had brought German friends one day and asked if they could show the lady the kitchen. She was obviously most intrigued by the whole place. When I took the tea I told them something that I had overheard one February in Tenerife. We were having tea out of doors in glorious hot sunshine having heard that day that snow was blanketing Europe. An obviously newly-arrived middle-aged couple came to share our table and the husband, looking round with expansive satisfaction, said to his wife, "Genau so wie in Köln." (Just like it is in Cologne.) I could not help smiling, he was delighted, but unfortunately the stumbling conversation soon came to an end on my side.

My trouble is that I am too lazy. But not as lazy as some English people living in Wales who will not pronounce place names properly. Many, for example, do not know that on the word 'newydd' the first syllable has the 'e' like that in 'never' and the double d is a soft 'th'. Margaret who helped me for so long gave me no peace once she discovered my ability to mimic. Every place name had to be pronounced correctly until, much to her amusement, I found myself correcting the pronunciation of the visitors.

Do not, however, believe too implicitly the Welshman who says that his language is a phonetic one. What about the 'y' in Gwynant and in Clynnog? There are some nasty traps for the Englishman who in his little learning may be tempted to be more Welsh than the Welsh. All the same it is worth a little trouble and the welcome you receive in country parts will certainly repay you. If you are not sure if a person is Welsh wait till he says 'please'. The 'ea' is not a diphthong that the Welshman recognises so he will say 'ple-ase'.

Many visitors enjoy encountering a strange language spoken within our shores. They buy a pocket Welsh dictionary from us to help identify place and house names. How exciting for the amateur historian to find a village called Betws Garmon, the grove or chapel of St Germain, who was sent to Wales to combat the Arian heresy, itself of Welsh origin. He was an effective and tireless preacher and teacher. About ten miles nearer Caernarfon a village has the name Cae Athraw, the field of the teacher. Probably no connection. In Wales the local people are happy to help out with meanings. In many parts of Scotland they cannot do so having lost the language entirely.

I know very little Welsh and few phrases beyond 'Dinner is ready' and 'What would you like to drink?' The latter I have learnt from hearing mothers ask their children at teatime. Teatime drinks are likewise a problem when newly arrived *au pair* and exchange girls are confronted with the awful reality of English afternoon tea. We do not offer coffee in the afternoon as all the gas jets are covered with trays of teapots and we do not always like to offer the instant variety to foreigners.

I recently found a family trying in vain to extract her wishes from a recently arrived French girl. Mamma tried *à boire* which did not work so Papa added *pour boire* which, if she recognised it, would convey something rather odd. Getting tired of waiting I stepped in with *comme boisson* which seemed to flurry her more than ever. For by this time she was probably uncertain what language was being hurled at her. It finally transpired that her choice was a fruit drink, but whether this was *citron* or *limonade* no one seemed quite sure. In any case she probably failed to recognise what we brought her.

Many foreign girls gaze with horror at the spread that is put before the family, and much to the relief of the younger English members decide to play safe with a shake of the head and "No t'ank you". No doubt hunger later on wears down their resistance.

The woman who taught me cookery had an annoying habit of accusing people of being behind the door when eyes and ears were given out. If you run a shop like mine you are reluctantly forced to the conclusion that many people have been denied their fair share where eyes are concerned. They will pick up a brooch with perhaps a stone in it, or engraved with a pattern and put it back upside down with only the pin and the price showing. For that was probably all that interested them. And this does not happen just once, on some days one may go round and find five or six items treated in the same way.

On another occasion an orange or terracotta coloured pot will be picked up and put back amongst the pink things. Displays based on colours in a picture or picking out those in a vase of flowers are a way of increasing the attractiveness of the goods themselves, while giving the customer an idea of how the things will look with their own colour schemes. But efforts of this kind are nullified if the customer jumbles things up as they feel inclined.

Perhaps in this particular instance it is I who am guilty of a blind eye. Are not pink and orange – the brighter the better – now blended as the latest style interior? Perhaps I have got into a rut and am holding on too long. The shops in the large towns certainly administer some shocks in these times. And yet so many of the young people one knows will have none of it and go in search of antiques instead.

On the other hand the colours known as 'sludge' and 'bottom of the pond' cannot be very inspiring to live with especially when glazed onto a mug that weighs your hand down empty and must be positively

81

arm-breaking when full. So pottery buying at the moment is not too easy unless you want to rename your place 'The Garret' or 'The Cellar'.

After a slight spell of depression, however, I return to my good spirits, remembering that there are always people looking for pleasant pieces to fit in with what they have. And there are all the charming and colourful modern pots as well, which cannot be completely overpowered by the dim and the dull.

Some of the most delightful gaily coloured pottery comes from Scandinavia, and it is flame-proof. One of the agents showed me a deep plate in this ware and averred that he cooked his breakfast bacon on one every day, and not just on an Aga hot plate, but on a gas light. I am afraid it needed a customer who found a piece in my shop which rounded out her collection, to persuade me to try it. The piece I selected was a small lidded casserole which had failed to sell as a butter dish. Gay daisy heads decorated the rim and the lid. Now it bubbles happily on my gas with peas or carrots for one, bread sauce, apple sauce; all the things which would normally have to be dished from a pan.

If I were a real business woman I should stock it seriously and have a demonstration pot cooking on a *calor* ring. Perhaps I will do so one day. Probably a good notice printed in the script I use would be as effective. This is a useful black letter alphabet I learnt as a student. A customer gave it a name last year rather to my surprise.

I have found such notices work on other occasions. Some odd-shaped dishes that I rashly bought when 'contemporary' was all the rage, had at one time seeped to the back of the cupboard. I labelled them tomato dish. They sold immediately though one lady called my bluff and asked, "Why tomatoes?" I replied, "They would probably do as well for cherries," and managed to keep a straight face. In the same way two dark brown slip ware bowls with honey-coloured edges sold quickly when labelled 'Prune bowls'. I have one which makes the dark fruit look even more appetising. People who have no ideas of their own have to have ideas given to them.

And yet how very rarely is anything given away! One has to remember the well known story of the tins in a grocery store which refused to sell at 9d each, and melted like snow when put into a crate and labelled 3 for 2/3d.

Notices do, however, occasionally seem to give people the wrong ideas. I have come to mistrust their ability to convey information because so few people read them correctly. On a notice in the window I once announced that we were open every weekday, at the times given below. While we were having lunch there one day a group of women looked in and one read aloud, "Open every Wednesday." As none of her companions troubled to correct her, I left her in ignorance too.

Perhaps one misunderstanding was wilful, for a young *paterfamilias* offered me a shilling for a pot of tea for four. When I asked for the other three shillings he pointed to the notice in the hall where he read 'pot of tea 1/–'. Because I had left out the 'each' he assumed presumably, that when serving large numbers, we really did turn into the charitable institution that some mothers of small children mistake us for. He was not at all the 'ivory tower' type of which we get a fair number in late August or September. Rather, I would have put him down as a normal technician or bank clerk. I must have been mistaken. He was surely on his way to his first million. To achieve it he was wisely applying two different sets of criteria, one for the paying and the other for the receiving end of business. Many of us do it to some extent but we do not all take it to these lengths.

Of one kind of Austrian pottery that we used to stock I would like to know the subsequent history for it seems to have disappeared from circulation. Though factory-made it was delightfully hand-painted on a white tin glaze. The various flowers might be a little stylised for they belonged to an almost peasant tradition, but this was brushwork and from that it took its character. Using a brush on a pot before it is fired is a little like painting on silk and something of this brushwork had an almost Chinese quality. A certain twist of the brush made a foxglove bell, the shape of the brush alone – probably a Japanese one – made daisy petals, and a wider sweep for a fat peony would use up the paint leaving part of the petals paled by the background showing through. Colours were clear, soft and amazingly varied and included greens, good pinks and lichen yellows which are not often found on pottery.

There were no black outlines for if brushwork is good an outline is an impertinence.

A Bangor agent stocked it for a time and I was able to go and choose my own; delightful plates that people could hang on narrow walls, flower pots, vases, powder bowls with lids in three sizes. Later I found only a London agent showing them and ordered a good supply of the plates as well as other pieces. To my horror I found that the factory had apparently lost its fine paintbrushes, or the best stuff was being kept for home consumption or for Germany, and only the second grade was finding its way to this country. They did not sell as before, of course. The people who cared found nothing of interest any more and for the ones who wanted something bright they were not garish enough. Now no agent stocks them. Has the pottery discovered its mistake and no longer sells in this country because agents refuse to have their fingers burnt twice? Some day I may find out.

A similar sort of thing happened when I bought some quite pleasant vases – or should we call them all containers? – from an English firm. Most of the pottery displayed in their main room, they told me, was for the South American market. It was frankly eye-hurting. In a little room off this chamber of horrors was a small collection of pleasant ware in greys, soft greens and oyster shades with contrasting linings. My order was as usual a modest one and, as I found the vases went well with flowers and sold well, the next February I went back for more. When I asked why they had used the hectic colours for linings which now quite ruined them, they said that they had decided the pots needed 'pepping up a bit'. No doubt their order books were a good deal healthier than the year before, though my name did not figure in them. I wondered if they would not have been wiser to cater for a small market for one more year at least, hoping to break new ground as well as getting repeat orders. After all, their bouncing South American sales could have financed the experiment many times over. But that is not the way industry is run.

How it is run and what goes on in the Potteries is a revelation. This is, of course, inevitable, fashion being what it is. But it means that a firm rarely has more than three years' harvest from a new idea before the hounds are after it. What they produce is never an exact copy, but anyone used to buying for a shop can recognize whence the idea has come. My suggestion of a three-year period during which a new idea is safe, is probably an optimistic one. People in the trade would be inclined to whittle the three down to one.

However, on the subject of 'adaptation', a recent trade show has provided considerable encouragement. The English potters have suddenly come to life with some splendid designs. There is a sameness in them as they are all, to use an artist's cliché, derivative. They derive, however, from something very well suited to repeat designs on 'flat and hollow-ware' as the makers un-poetically describe plates and cups. Most examples show a varied repeat of a fairly compact semi-abstract motif varied with a smaller one of with 'connective tissue'.

Cups and saucers have never looked happy with flowers and fruits growing round or across them. This too naturalistic style led in the late thirties to the horrible idea of square plates. Here one of the rules of arithmetic was being broken. For if a shape well adapted to the production methods which a material imposes, has to be considerably changed to accommodate the decoration decided on, then that form of decoration is fundamentally unsuitable. The square plate was posing as a picture for it is with pictures that naturalistic flower drawings are normally associated. Square dishes, when they are made, are of fairly thick earthenware to resist loss of shape in the kiln. Successful decoration on these is rarely floral.

Posies are a very different matter and charming ones have decorated both English and Continental china for long enough. Growing sprays have also been used most successfully by Chinese potters for centuries. Would it be begging the question to point out that these sprays were often in the hands of superb artists? It might be mentioned too that such sprays were not naturalistic. They submitted to a discipline, a convention, which in a very subtle way made them suitable for the use to which they were put.

At the moment, however, people are imposing most interesting and often highly successful disciplines on nature in the new art of flower arrangement. They are also hanging reproductions of superb botanical drawings on their walls; or they are doing their own flower painting. On their pots they want something different.

The result of this is at last a choice of crisp cheerful designs in greens, blues and reds as well as the ubiquitous browns, yellows, oranges and blacks, designs which blend happily with rooms both traditional and modern. Some exhibit more growth and rhythm than others. In some the isolated motifs are actually united to form a rich and flowing band. Some have an almost Adam flavour. But nearly all display, what has been a trifle lacking in English commercial pottery design for some years, not only verve and pleasant contrast, but also dignity.

After thus eulogising non-naturalistic design in pottery, I may, in one of my recent orders for Welsh pottery, lay myself open to an accusation of inconsistency. I very much liked some flat and shallow dishes in their soft self-colours, decorated with flower drawings. To increase the apparent flouting of rules I would add that the flowers were naturalistic. But the best of them had beside good design which fitted them to the shape, the subtle naturalism of botanical studies. In these an artist, though he may appear to be copying exactly, nevertheless makes those small emphases which in fact bring the drawing to life. Moreover the decorations were in monochrome, to use a technical term they were *sgraffito*. That is they were 'drawn' in the coloured slip. This technique, by exploiting the very character of the product to provide the decoration, gave them a truly ceramic quality.

It is indeed the amazing variety and resource that occurs in technical products in this country that makes our arts and crafts so interesting. The atmosphere of the applied arts is certainly a lively one. And there are in my opinion too many people running down everything to do with English cookery to allow, without a struggle, another happy band to glorify in house décor, everything that can go by the name of Scandinavian.

Their furniture and tableware look charming when well displayed in our shops. But what is it like to live with exclusively? Perhaps the experience of an Englishwoman who lived in Finland for nearly a year may give us an idea. At first everything seemed so refreshing, so clean and beautifully simple and, though firmly traditional, not lacking in imagination. After a time, however, a conviction that the art of everyday things was certainly aseptic gave way to a suspicion that it was, in some measure, a trifle dead.

Perhaps an analogy from that delicious dish, the English steak pie, would help at this point. In Finland, if they had steak pie the pastry would be crisp and delicious and withal well risen. So the meat underneath had presumably boiled once to produce the raising steam. The filling represented a good healthy tradition but something had gone wrong somewhere. For when you cut into the lovely crust you found that the meat was only lukewarm.

Compare the English product. In the inside of the English pie you may find what the pundits abhor, gravy. The meat has probably come from the other side of the world, paid for by the output of English 'art ware' factories. But there is no doubt about its being hot. It is bubbling up and, against all the rules, it is here and there pleasantly soaking into the pastry.

For in England we are not living purely on one tradition nor are we hidebound by 'good taste'. Some of the lesser known firms are the most fecund of ideas. It is indeed not always realised that the jugs, round casseroles, teapots and many more things produced by a family firm in the forefront of design, are all thrown by hand in stoneware clay. The output and accuracy of their throwers is truly magic. Also, an original woman designer having purchased one of the old-fashioned potteries had been in the vanguard of new ideas. She has discovered the vitality that can still be found embedded in Victorian taste. It is in finding germs of newness within an old conception that a designer shows his or her mettle, for very little is really new, most is inspired adaptation. But the inspiration must be there.

The seconds, which one firm produces occasionally, instead of finding their way on to the market stalls, are used up in an original way. They are not imperfect in shape being only glazing casualties, and after re-glazing with white they are decorated with brushwork. They have great freshness and vigour and fill a definite gap. Most are very pleasant, though some designs are too 'full of meat' and, of that bogey of the English pottery decorator, dark lines.

So in this country you may buy pottery made at stately homes, or if you prefer it, auctioned on a market stall. You can also, if you trouble to look, find it in any market town this output of individualists who are something of ceramic artists, as well as the products of factories whose owners were pioneers two hundred years ago. You 'pays your money' and not too much of it either, 'and you takes your choice'. Healthier I think on the whole.

But enough of pottery for there must be some people, strange thought, who are not interested in it. To round out the stock and make it more interesting there are the delightful pieces of stainless steel handmade in the Lake District. They sell with encouraging regularity as do other handmade things, amongst them the hand block printed head scarves and aprons. The head scarves are made in cotton muslin so are ideal for summer as they do not slip like silk and being triangular instead of square they do not make a bulky knot. I used to find them doubtful sellers because folded up they do not reveal their charms. Draped and tied on a stiff foundation, however, they are quite a different matter. Being an artistic production there are no design numbers to quote for repeats, so the best must be picked out of each selection sent, and returned to be copied. They have taken a long time to produce a really good blue, always a popular colour, but their yellows, greys, greens and dull reds are delightful. I now stock far more of them than I used to and sell them steadily. They are made by disabled girls, some of them working against enormous difficulties, as I saw when I visited their place in Hampshire. So making an effort to sell more of them seems to be doubly worthwhile.

Rush work is another craft product that sells well when made into shopping and wastepaper baskets, but I would rather be at the retail than the production end of this little industry.

It is fraught with difficulties for the craft has to be learnt, and trained workers have a way of leaving just when their assistance begins to be valuable. A West Country source of charming light-weight baskets – of which I took care to secure two for myself – completely dried up and I could extract no more from the maker. Asking the reason I was told that she could no longer make enough for resale and found that it paid her better to go round agricultural shows and sell direct.

An East Anglian source of supply became precarious for different reasons. The river from which the rushes used to be obtained had been cleaned so that in the swift water the rushes no longer thrive so they have to be imported from the continent. It is interesting to notice how the weather affects these baskets. Culled in a dry summer the rushes tend to be stubble gold, after a wet one shades of lichen green predominate.

Trays are to be had in splendid variety at present. One type which I have sold for thirty years is in plain wood, chiefly oak and walnut, good looking, durable and heat and alcohol resistant. Melamine, a plastic which is allowed to impregnate a wood fibre base under pressure, is completely reliable and good for all types of plain and decorative trays. Fibre glass enables actual materials to be stiffened and made into a durable tray which has the added advantage of a slightly rough surface to discourage slipping.

These trays are, however, a slight disappointment to me because I thought when I first saw them that lovely things would follow. Knowing the wonderful ranges of cretonnes that are to be had one tends to be disappointed at the narrowness of the choice selected for these. Perhaps some of the best fabrics are protected by copyright. I do not think this can be the reason, because pleasant designs are used but not enough of them.

Probably as usual it is the customer, or the maker's idea of the customer, who influences the choice. With my customers there are a few tried favourites and I often wonder where the rest go. My own choice which looks lovely with old furniture and soft-coloured cretonnes is, not surprisingly, to be discontinued. I bought several trays in this design last year and certain people, as I expected, were delighted to find them and would not look at any others.

There is certainly a plethora of pleasant things to be had nowadays and it is sometimes refreshing to look back from these days of plenty to those of relative shortage. In those days of rationing I sold soft toys, and soft toys to me mean little ninety-year-old Mrs Lilley who stayed with me and helped me with everything, not least by making me feel that life, even in wartime was well worth living. She walked round the sea edge with me, nothing daunted by the narrow, uneven and winding paths strewn often with brambles and edged with fragrant roses.

In her spare time and using clothing coupons for the fur fabric, she made rabbits stuffed with kapok. For their eyes she needed boot buttons, no longer to be had in the big towns. With what delight did she find a post office in a Welsh village which had a drawer full of them.

I also had cause to bless a draper's shop in our little town. In those days I made oblong hessian shopping bags. The braid that covered the handles was carried down to the bottom thereby dividing the area into three parts which admitted further decoration with lovely braid in other colours. Tans, rusts and greens were available in the hessian and I amused myself finding braids to go with them. When I had bought up their entire stock of braid my little shop, hoping to be useful and with no doubt other hopes in mind offered me brush braid 'in case I could use it'. Rick rack braid made an effective decoration for the bags. I came across several craft workers in those days and we were only too glad to get hold of anything. Even felt work and sealing wax work had a ready sale. One lady made most effective posies from beechnuts which she dyed in various colours. She also used rick rack braid for her craft work and being deaf she had a way of going into a shop and enquiring "Have you any riff raff?"

What a jump from those days to these when even the dolls have everything they need. For about four years we stocked all equipment for dolls from skates to swim caps through Brownie uniforms and riding habits. It was great fun for us as well as for the children. If toys like these have had only a very short stay the clipped wool ones have been part of my stock for nearly thirty years and they were being made long before I opened the café. The original maker retired and, unaccountably, was unable to sell her business or even persuade her workers to carry on. However, her energetic agent after a few years found another weaver in another part of the country who was willing to take the little industry under his roof. Some of the skilled workers were found to be willing to move so the animals are being made once more.

I sometimes hear people say, "Oh yes, they are quite easy, you know, you just wrap wool round and round." But at that point they seem to stop, for they realise as well as I do that it is the bushy tail and tiny well-formed paws as well as the ears, carefully cut from felt that give life and character to the squirrels, while white mice have the beadiest of eyes and pink felt ears.

One of these mice had worked hard for over a year. I was told by an anxious aunt who came in one afternoon late in the season. It had given comfort to her little nephew who had gone to sleep every night with the little morsel clutched in his hand. Now his little friend was pretty well 'sans everything', so when the boy heard that his aunt was coming to north Wales, he asked her to call and get a new one for him. Luckily there was one left. So, while I rushed for her change, she went out to watch for the 'bus, which obligingly stopped outside the house for her. 'Buses still do that in Wales.

Mary Howe's sketch of the Bobbing Boats café

Chapter V

'Helpers' or Staff

If you can keep your head when all about you
Are losing theirs and blaming it on you.
From the poem *If—* by Rudyard Kipling

I do not actually quote these lines when replying to letters of enquiry about possible summer jobs. But I always hope that the applicant realises what faces her. For busy wet mornings and fine afternoons require a good deal of concentration.

In a small place where trade is seasonal there is only a background of long-term people who can cope efficiently with sales. A good deal has to be left to the students, few of whom come for more than three weeks, though they occasionally repeat the experiment two years running. They need a cool head and fortunately most of them realise that recrimination never got a member of staff anywhere. It is often those who are inefficient themselves who bounce into the kitchen saying, "Who's done so-and-so?" One woman who came for the summer had a habit of doing this. She also had a habit of picking up any teapot she might find to hand, instead of waiting for the freshly brewed one to be given to her. But the students are far more 'on the spot' than this.

In any case does it matter who may have done 'so-and-so'? The important thing is to avoid the occasion for the same mistake in the future. And that, as I see it is the job of the boss.

Small details can make for the avoidance of mistakes. It is for this reason that customers find it odd when we do not appear to welcome their attempts at helping us. Whether all the people who pop their heads round the kitchen door and say "Tea for four, please", are really intending to help us I do not know. I think they often like to see what is going on in the 'orderly chaos' which one customer called our kitchen. Many think they are saving time and our feet and we are grateful. But just as many imagine that they will thus get served immediately. They do not really mean to jump the queue, because they simply do not realise that there is one.

Difficulties can arise with a 'kitchen door' order, or one given in the hall to a student probably busy on something else. For one thing we do not know where they are sitting, though they may indicate this vaguely. And, were we to prepare their order immediately, even if theirs was the next in turn, we might arrive to find that the table needed to be cleared. What we should also probably find would be two children who wanted milk or fruit cordial to drink, instead of tea and a figure-conscious mother who did not want anything to eat.

Students soon see the sense of our rule that orders should be taken at the table, even if this involves a walk to the farthest table outside. However, a good team will see that this waitress does not go empty-handed but take hot water or cakes to another table on her way.

It is working things out in this way that is the fascination of waiting. And though we try to keep to our pre-decided tables we all help one another, and if one waitress has a quiet spell she goes to the aid of someone who is snowed under.

In most cafés the tables are numbered but with so many short-term helpers this is not practicable. Early in her training the student has to learn to differentiate the 'square table' from the 'back window'; to tell the 'oak seat', which is actually an elm love seat, in the big tea-room from the oak garden seat outside. The idea for this seat was actually given to me by the man who was doing the outside decorating. Up to then this space had been empty except when I grew a morning glory there in a pot. However the decorator had to move the other garden seat from beside the wall and he put it, for convenience on the left of the door. People promptly sat on it, either to wait for their turn or for their friends after tea. Next year I moved an oak garden seat that had been in the tea-room to this spot and acquired a new piece to take its place. A garden stool of the same type put by it does not impede entrance to the house and will accommodate tea for two.

Most of our difficulties and many of our muddles arise from the fact that in the busy season the place is not big enough for what we try to do in it. In the tiny larder there may be doubt as to the order in which cakes or fruit loaves have to be used. As I know I cannot be everywhere, I resort a good deal to labels. But I have learnt never to label anything 'use first'. I know full well that that particular cake will be still sitting on the shelf unseen at the end of the afternoon. Instead I label the dangerously fresh 'use last'. When the new has to be avoided and we know the older exists there is a fair chance of someone looking in the tin and finding it.

So, having taken, as I think, reasonable precautions I also take the blame for small misfortunes. What I have never been willing to take is the advice of many of my customers. For they want me to enlarge. But often many people see the café only at the busy season. The extra space is only needed for about six weeks. For the remaining twenty or so expansion would involve more walking and more floor to keep clean, neither of which I welcome.

Many people are amazed at what we do achieve in the space for we often serve a hundred teas in an afternoon. The service may not always be very prompt, but I know that on the whole we are considered to be fairly quick. Perhaps my obstinacy in resisting change is because it is the twenty less busy weeks that I really enjoy, looking on the six hectic ones as a sort of necessary evil. Though I know it is in the six weeks of scramble that most of the money is taken.

The money may, however, be taken, but it is not necessarily made. For when proportion is once more invoked I find that the ratio of takings to wages remains surprisingly constant throughout the season.

This is partly because in August we are working to capacity and many would-be customers are unfortunately turned away at the end of the afternoon or are unable to find a seat earlier. It is, however, also true that the proportion of sales to catering is much lower in the busy weeks. After a hectic August afternoon we may find we have sold virtually nothing. A hot morning in June, by contrast, may bring old customers, seeking the shade and ready to buy their presents for the year.

It is for these people that I like to keep the place small and unchanged. They have been coming to me for years, many of them have seen housing developments at home, established shops posing as supermarkets and petrol pumps where gardens used to be. To them the Bobbing Boats is a sign of continuity, of the old order which in at least one loved spot, has not as yet had to yield its place to new.

It is to these people also that we are so grateful for all the help and consideration they give us. They are so patient and, if they happen to see more than one waitress, they take such pains to see that their orders are not duplicated. It is partly because of this feeling of cooperation that running a café in a small holiday place is so rewarding. We are indeed lucky, for people on holiday are usually in a good mood, even if it is raining.

Customers, however, would be surprised at the amount of energy a wet spell takes out of us. For some reason, even if one does not try to cheer people up, one feels in a way responsible. Hope for fine days, too long deferred, can make the café owner's heart as sick as that of the holiday-maker, having his one fortnight of the year at the sea. But he can go home. She is left to try to hold out better hopes for the next batch. How little people know, who try to maintain that I like bad weather because they say it brings more trade.

Good weather or bad, the gentlemen delight in teasing the students especially one who may be unwise enough to let it be known that she cannot add up. In any case this has usually been guessed already. For most employers know that the rising generation cannot give the answer to twelve at four pence halfpenny without recourse to much arithmetic.

And what of those students who help us out in the summer? Who are they and where do they come from? One, Nancy, an art student who came to me some years ago is now doing museum work. Her mother had been at school with me. The first year Nancy brought a friend who was studying drama in London. She has since appeared on TV on Sunday evenings. She had many interesting things to tell us of her training.

Nancy's companion the next year was from a Quaker family, one member of which had helped Dr. Schweitzer at Lambarene. The next year I received a letter from a girl whose family had stayed for many years at the same seaside house as Nancy's family. She said she knew the café well. Only when she arrived with her brother and sister did I realise from whom the letter had come. For as long, it seemed, as I could remember wet mornings in early summer, her parents had come with their growing family for five hot chocolates. Her first appearance was when she was eighteen months old. Two years with her and two friends were followed by one with her younger sister. Last year a friend of hers came with a relative and so it goes on, or I hope it will.

They usually come two together for company as it makes a better holiday for them. Most of them, however, do not look upon it merely as a holiday. In fact the only really unsatisfactory pair I have had were, quite obviously from the beginning, interested solely in their tennis and boating. They went home after two weeks as we could manage better without them. Most students, however, take the job quite seriously but manage to enjoy themselves at the same time.

The fact that one girl found herself not entirely successful at the café work was not really her own fault. To start with she was an artist and I find that artists are not observant. By that I mean they do not concern themselves solely with the obvious things that interest the rest of the world. For theirs is a private world. While they are trying very hard to be what they think we consider efficient the truly practical type can take in the whole kitchen at one glance. Yet after three weeks the artist may not have discovered that the spare stock of milk is kept for coolness by the back door.

Life was being made difficult for this girl, however, by the fact that she was at an unsuitable art school. A huge pile of vacation homework, which she only partly understood, was weighing on her mind and impairing her concentration. After one or two afternoons when she had been so muddled that we had to 'carry her', it was decided that I should pay her a little less and she should help in the mornings with the biscuits, which she did very well, and do her homework in the afternoons. I heard afterwards that she had changed to another art school and had done very well. I knew her school art mistress having met her when serving on the jury in Caernarfon.

I find that it often helps us to work harmoniously with the students if I use my imagination to discover why they have taken a holiday job. The money is an obvious reason, for they may be saving up to go abroad, but there are other reasons.

One girl told me at the start of her stay that she would like to 'get domesticated'. I knew then just where I was. I suggested that three weeks was a short time for the process, but her taking me into her confidence showed me that she was willing to learn and did not mind being told of mistakes.

I always advise them to ask as many questions as they like, as I prefer answering questions to having things done wrong. But people lacking in confidence – and I was one myself – are the very ones who pretend to have it and hate to appear dependent. So I tend to stay around at biscuit-making time, at least for the first few days. In this way I have been able to rescue more than one batch that has made a bad start, though quick action has had to be backed up by a pencil and paper calculation. However, nothing but a little time has been wasted.

Some girls of undoubted scholastic ability take a job of this sort to prove to themselves that they are not fools in the house because they have had little time or encouragement to practise at home. And less clever girls who have brilliant sisters like to round off their experience and give themselves much needed confidence. Many of them, too, are keen to do a little baking for I always warn them that they are not coming purely as waitresses. I need their help with making the biscuits.

It was from the Anglesey café that I took the idea of serving biscuits as well as cakes for afternoon tea and also with morning coffee. Biscuits on the menu make another piece of 'dove-tailing' possible, for if you unexpectedly have a slack afternoon one helper can make a batch of shortbreads.

In the quieter part of the season we do this more and more. If you find the right kind of people to help and work up an atmosphere of getting on and enjoying the work, no one wants to merely wait around. This spare-time baking was started by the toy-makers, neither of whom could bear to be idle. One of them had been a nurse and informed me soon after she arrived that she always liked to finish a job and hated to be broken off it when she was interested. I told her that, as she had a tea-shop in mind as an adjunct to their toy-making, I felt she would have to change her attitudes. She did so completely and became as good a 'dove-tailer' as I could have wished.

The shortbread recipe that I brought from Anglesey was very rich. I had to change it when rationing came along and did not like the result so I began to make flapjacks instead.

Then a friend of two of my helpers wrote to say that she would like to come and work part-time, helping with the baking and going sailing and walking in the afternoons. She added that as her mother was one of the best cooks in Derbyshire she would bring her own recipes!

"What a cheek!" I thought, but I accepted the offer all the same. My present-day shortbread, which is in reality a German biscuit as it contains egg, was a recipe she brought and very grateful I was for it. Instead of rolling it out we press it into tins and cut it while it is cooling. I vary it from time to time by adding chopped walnuts or finely crushed cornflakes. And from it I have at last evolved a Quaker oat biscuit that I like.

The other favourite biscuit is only for those who like coconut. Originally the coconut and oats in it were in equal quantities, but one day found us short of coconut. Not to be put off I used what I had, and increased the quantity of oats. We like it even better since the alteration and it is also cheaper! In fact hardly a year goes by without some adaptation, or alteration being made.

Making biscuits enables me to have help with the baking. With the rubbing in of the scone mix and the mixing of the bread flour it occupies the students until coffee time. For some of them it is rather a trial at first and it is not necessarily the domestic science students who do it best. In their case I have to give a warning that I break a great many rules in the interests of speed. So they have to forget what they do in my kitchen when they go back to college or start teaching. Many of them have come to me through my knowing a member of the staff at their college.

Girls who like cooking are welcome; those who are fond of tidying up are even more so. I usually know when I have a good 'slabber' on the staff, for when the two of us are busy in the kitchen at the end of the evening the second student will be found quietly engrossed in the larder, wiping down all the slabs and finding the odd shelf which before her arrival had probably been sadly neglected. The name we took over from Anglesey. A friend who helped there used to say,

"Anyone can wash up, it is only those who do the 'slabs' afterwards who make a proper job of it."

I know I am unorthodox. A friend once told me I was the best unorthodox cook she knew. But she did not mean it as a compliment for amongst other things she had been a teacher of cookery. She certainly did not think much of my cooking one day when she found a half-ounce weight in her shortbread. It was the old recipe in which the fat was simply rubbed in and the crumbs pressed into the tin. Each tin had to contain fifteen and a half ounces of mixture so I put the odd half ounce weight onto the scale pan. On one occasion it found its way into the finished article. It was, perhaps, a good thing that I adopted the Derbyshire recipe! And what luck that it should happen to a friend who knew me and my odd ways.

Though I have so much appreciated the help of resident students in the past, and have learnt a great deal from the experience of young people in the house, yet I have decided that for the future, I will depend more and more on girls who live or stay in the district. Healthy appetites call for a good deal of cooking and shopping, and though I have usually escaped the food fad, all this house-work is a tiresome extra at the busiest time of the year. Moreover, my friends are now reaching retirement age too, so they will be able to come and stay and give a hand. And as I get older I am handing the evening coffee trade more and more over to people whose feet are younger than mine.

Foreign students seem to get into the way of things wonderfully quickly though I have to warn them that in Wales they will have less practice in hearing English spoken in shops and buses than they would do in England.

A Czech girl who helped us had a very good command of English. We were, however, surprised at what she came out with one day. A family had – as families do – sent a few members on ahead to secure a table. Gradually more drifted in until an order, apparently for three, finally ended up as more than twice that number. "These people," announced Greta, as she came into the kitchen, "they multiply like rabbits."

She had got away from Europe before the war and had much of interest to tell us of her life in Czechoslovakia where she worked in a shop. Hours were very long, but she said, "we did not seem to get through as much in the day as you do in England. I think it is the organisation. You English are known to be excellent organisers." A considerable crumb of comfort to us, who are always running ourselves down, I thought.

Some of the students have been Welsh-speaking. One of them told me that when she was sweeping outside one morning the dustmen arrived and she heard one of them saying, "Why is Cwm Pennant so beautiful and the life of man so short?" One can hardly imagine an English dustman quoting poetry. He might say, "Oh to be in England, now that April's there," while chafing his hands on an un-salubrious morning of that 'cruellest month'. But would he know it was poetry?

When your house is used as a workshop, the law requires you to install a first aid kit. I have complied but we rarely use the apparatus I bought, though I have added to the endless little rolls of burn dressing and the bottles of iodine and *sal volatile*, and other more useful items.

Instead we keep handy a clean bandage and a bottle of homeopathic hypericum. I like to think that this was named St John's Wort by the Knights of St John who ran, first in Rhodes and then in Malta for hundreds of years, hospitals famed for their cleanliness and efficiency.

We tend to think that our forefathers were pathetically ignorant of medicine. But it is obvious that wounds must have been successfully healed in those days. Did not Raleigh live for over 30 years after receiving a serious leg wound at Cadiz?

Mrs Ward, who helped in the kitchen, was not interested in arguments of this kind but she had no doubts of the efficiency of our hypericum which she always referred to as 'that stuff'. It healed her many cuts and burns and she would often take some of the lotion home with her and show me its good effects next day.

For colds both Lilian and I use cinnamon. Lilian uses the household form mashed in hot water, while I use the proprietary essence. Many days' work has this enabled us to do when otherwise we should have been laid low. It is surprising the number of students whom we have had to dose more or les forcibly. They prefer to leave a cold to take its course. As this usually means handing it on to customers too, I do not allow them to do waiting while they are in the infectious stage. They have to be 'Background Bessie' instead. That makes them swallow the cinnamon if nothing else will! It is in the early stages that it works best.

Being 'Background Bessie' involves chiefly clearing and setting trays, putting out cakes, washing cutlery and, nowadays, keeping an eye on Fred the dishwasher. We try to encourage everyone to be as self-supporting as possible in the way of putting out food, so that they do not always have to wait for us to do it.

When they first begin we always smile at one another as we see them dive into the larder to put out the cakes as soon as they have given us their order. There, I know, they feel they are safe, they can think out what they are supposed to be doing in peace, with no one to watch. But the cakes are usually the last thing needed so the poor girl is called back into the kitchen, to clear and reset her tray and collect the food she needs. We all try to arrange our trays in more or less the same way, so that anyone glancing at them can see what is missing. With a little care, afternoon tea for two can all be taken in one journey, instead of the seven that two of my helpers counted when they went to another café for tea on their day off. Tea for three is possible too though we may have to come back later for the cakes. When we are very busy I resort to a little trick about the cakes and say to the people as I serve their tea. "Will you ask someone when you are ready for your cakes?" By doing this I put the onus of remembering onto them. For a surprising number of people will say that they have not had any cakes, because they thought there weren't any, while all the tables around them have had their board. I find that to put them out on boards instead of plates, flatters the cakes considerably and people like to see them so, because they look 'different'. We try to make a point also of taking the cakes later if there are children, because it saves the mother trouble. If no cakes are in sight there can be no argument about 'bread and butter first'.

Even our method of picking up and putting down the trays presents difficulty to the students at first, for we hold them by their long sides. This facilitates passing through narrow doorways and passages. It also reduces muscle fatigue because the arms, being lightly pressed to the sides, are partly supported. But it is the neck and shoulder muscles which feel the most relief. The new habit takes only a day or so to acquire. After that the awkward conventional one is happily forgotten.

I have often had tea, particularly in a hotel, brought on a huge tray and nothing whatever has been done to arrange the crocks. The over-worked waiter, with no one else to deal with, has simply left us to sort things out for ourselves. Yet when we take tea and cakes for two in this way with the crocks for each person arranged so that all that remains for the pourer to do is to hand her companion her tea and her plate, people seem quite dumbfounded. Many take everything off the tray, unless we warn them, and put the hot teapot down on the polished table. When all they want to eat is biscuits or cakes it is a great saving of time for us to be able simply to put the tray down in front of them.

Another time-saver is, however, also a memory-teaser. On many occasions a waitress is just preparing to sail out of the kitchen when another pair of eyes has noticed an omission,. "Butter balls," she calls after her and slips a little dish onto the tray just in time. Instead of buttering the scones we have, of late, begun to serve the butter separately. We found a gadget left from years ago for making tiny butter pats, as I hoped, quickly. However it had too many parts and for some reason the ring and the plunger never seemed to be in alignment. The substitute which we bought at a cost of six shillings had a short life. The first time it was used the working part flew off and was never seen again. Now we use the ring part of the old one without the plunger. We find that a tiny bottle which once held homoeopathic pills does the job far better.

What labour-saving idea shall we find for next year? Perhaps we shall find none. Our wholesale grocery suppliers have come up with one already, however, for they tell me that they will in future only make deliveries or orders over the value of five pounds. It seems that I shall have to re-organise, not only my storage space but my memory also. How does one set about doing that?

The Upstairs Sitting Room – a painting by Mary Howe

Chapter VI

More Customers

Archbishop Temple at ordinands' tea party: "Ah Mr Smith, take a chair and have some tea." Ordinand: "Watkins-Smith, Sir." Archbishop: "Then take two chairs."

When many years ago, at the doorway of a small café in the Lake District, my sister and I were met by the owner with a request to sit at a table for two, I could not help feeling that she might have been better employed, for she was asking us to do what we were intending to do in any case.

This happened while I was looking round for somewhere to start a café myself. I knew from my experience in Anglesey that people who come to cafés are, on the whole, reasonable and considerate.

At the Bobbing Boats we are too busy to play the floor usher. If customers are few there is always something to claim our attention somewhere. As we take the orders, however, we try to arrange people either to our own advantage or to their greater comfort. We do not always succeed.

I quite often have to invite people to take a window table because they feel that their small numbers are not justified in occupying one. The window tables are, in fact, little bigger than some others, but we put as many chairs round them as possible knowing that they are the most popular.

If people are accommodating they are also surprisingly blind, or are they merely gregarious? I am never quite sure. Often two lots of people will come in and choose the left-hand room. A third family will drift in after them and will be surprised when I tell them that there is a window table in the other room. If there are children they will notice it, the grownups merely go where they see others. So true is this that a friend, when she first started her café, used to ask her mother to sit in the window and drink a cup of tea. She was soon joined by others.

Our policy of letting people sit where they like sometimes results in every one of the eight tables being 'engaged' though in fact each is occupied by only two people. And we can accommodate over thirty-six in the house. Our tactics on such occasions depend on situations unknown to the customer. We may, for example, have been caught napping, expecting the grey and uninviting day to prove a quiet one. Or people may have come early before our local helpers have arrived or while the students are off-duty.

On such occasions I do not waste time arranging people, but say firmly that we are full. The narrowness of the hall will prevent the faint-hearted from finding the truth out for themselves. The more determined will find room and will share a table with others.

In the meantime there is a 'chase round' behind the scenes. More bread must be cut and buttered, more cakes cut up, trays set, milk and jam decanted, sugar bowls filled. For it is going to be a busy afternoon after all.

If we are well prepared or if the sudden invasion has been caused by a shower of rain, we resort to a different policy. People must then be re-arranged and some may have to be asked to move, frequently a delicate operation. Many customers are, however, quite willing to share a table provided someone is at hand to effect the introduction. Others do not even wait for one. By the end of tea we may find them chatting, often gainfully. They have been able to tell one another of places to visit and byways to explore. Some of the loveliest small roads are gated, however, and to recommend them may not always be wise in case the suggestion is followed in the busy days of August. Then, there may be up to five cars waiting at the various gates.

It must be borne in mind also that there are people who do not care to tell others of their finds. Their attitude is perhaps understandable. They may be like one family who, after taking holidays for years in the southwest, had at last found Borth-y-Gest. They ended their appreciation of it all by saying, "And when we get home, we shan't tell a soul."

Changes, we have found, may be made windowards, but not in the reverse direction; although people are willing enough to move from one window to another. I took such willingness rather too much for granted in the early war years and learnt my lesson.

Receiving an order for tea for one with a foreign accent, I had the temerity to ask the lady to move from her seat in the window to a small side table which we then had. She was probably a refugee, had suffered, or narrowly escaped suffering and was determined to secure all she could for the future, for she amazed me by replying, "No, I will not."

I knew full well what would soon happen, so I calmly put her tea on the small table and left her to it. A few minutes later families of children began to arrive. They certainly would not have left her in sole possession of the window table, so she owed her peaceful tea to my high-handed action. Nowadays I should have left her where she was, feeling that if she had to endure a noisy tea, she was only getting her deserts for her lack of consideration.

'Ones' are difficult and many of them know it, and on a busy day tend to be apologetic if not actually self-effacing. If the latter they run the risk of being forgotten altogether, though we really try to make them feel as welcome as anyone else.

That they are not truly welcome everywhere I once gathered when I had lunch in a restaurant in Buxton. My table was near the serving hatch where the waitresses collected their orders and I could hear them exchanging notes. "I've had fourteen ones," announced my waitress in a tone of disgust. Well did I understand how she felt. But without me it would have been thirteen, perhaps even worse!

Travelling alone on the continent I have never been made to feel unwelcome in a restaurant. Raised eyebrows and *"Toute seule?"* have, however, greeted me in small hotels in France. And these were not the modern tourist hotels where single rooms are at a premium, but the modest variety that caters for 'commercials'.

Large parties also tend to feel nervous when they see the smallness of the tearooms. We have very few coaches; but occasionally people who know me bring a party from a holiday home.

On one such occasion the leader split up his flock taking the larger portion into the little room. My assistant dealt with them while I tackled the shepherd-less remnant in the larger one. The charade which followed – surely a word which has come from the Welsh word '*siarad*' to speak – was something like this:-

Self-appointed spokeswoman, looking anxiously round; "But there's eleven of us." I say: "Very well, and you would all like tea. Now how will you sit? Yes, you could sit seven in the window, but there are only six chairs." SAS: "But there's eleven of us." I: "Yes, that will be all right. I will bring a pot to start you off."

I then return to the kitchen and bring a pot for six which the SAS immediately realises cannot serve all, so she informs me again of their terrifying numbers. I reassure her and rush off for the pot for five already made and sitting on a tray with the crocks.

When I arrive it is to find only three people still needing to be served as the tenth and eleventh had all the time really belonged to the other room and had merely strayed in to look at the beads.

I comment on this, but one cheerful lady makes things easier by saying, "Never mind, I'll drink two lots, I'm ready for it, I must say."

We very rarely undertake to serve large parties because it is really unfair to other customers who may arrive at the same time. When I have on occasion agreed to provide tea for some organisation or society I have stipulated that it will be an afternoon tea only. In spite of my letter to the secretary and my quotation of the price many of the party have obviously been disappointed. For they still secretly hoped for a 'knife and fork tea'.

I once allowed myself to be persuaded to provide afternoon tea for the Dyserth and District Naturalists' Association on condition that they arrived early. They did, but, needless to say, on that day, so did the regular customers. Soon the place was seething with people, but I felt it was only fair to try to serve the naturalists first.

So I rather unwisely asked my young helper to try to get them seated and bring back numbers for tea. She went up to the first person she met in the hall and said, "Are you Dyserth and District?" The unfortunate lady; probably from Nottingham, had no idea what the girl was talking about and looked distinctly startled and the helper suddenly losing her nerve fled back to the kitchen. We then adopted a more reasonable plan and I made two pots of tea to go on the trays ready laid with food and crocks. Each bearing a tray we went into the tearoom announcing loudly; "This is tea for four for the Dyserth and District. Where shall I put it?" They soon spoke up and we got everyone served comfortably.

It would probably have been wiser to set enough tables for the naturalists in one room and usher them into there when they arrived. I have, however, known so many occasions on which people have failed to arrive at the time arranged that I feared lest this system might appear to be tempting providence.

People are often surprised that on a busy afternoon we cannot promise to reserve a table for them at, say, 4.15. The reason is that we cannot really afford to have tables standing vacant when they could be being used and it is not as easy to time people precisely as many people imagine. What we often do in the case of a family is to reserve the food for them and ask them to come later. They can then have a walk and come back to be served at once.

Messages, I have found, have a way of missing their way and I mistrust them now. My sister was once met as she came downstairs with a request for the right time so she said she would look at the kitchen clock. Arriving in the kitchen she asked a student to tell the gentleman in the hall that it was half past five. The student did so but it was the wrong man. This one had in fact slipped in wondering if it was too late for tea and took the student's statement as a confirmation of his fears. However, the right person overheard so no harm was done.

The customers that we find difficult are those we call the 'loud-voiced ones'. The voices in question are usually connected with the smartest of accents, but in a small place this does not make them any more welcome. Their owners often move about in fairly large numbers and they have a tendency to move the furniture and the flowers as well as themselves. In short, they 'take possession' and we are only too relieved when they also take their leave.

In early summer we find quite innocuous people will have moved the flowers and I am now prepared for this for I know that their reason is hay-fever. Our objection to moving the chairs is really accounted for by my lack of wisdom when years ago I decided that I could bear the dark door frames no longer. Instead of having the paint burnt off I put light paint on top of the dark. And even when the hall was properly decorated years later this process was repeated. The result is that the slightest knock will chip off the paint. And if much moving of chairs is done during the summer we find that, when the crowds have thinned out and we can once more see the details of our surroundings, a horrible brown rash reveals itself in both doorways. Customers cannot be expected to be aware of such details and must often think us more than a little fussy and uncooperative.

The garden seat by the front door seems to invite strong men to remove it to other parts of the little *parterre*. As it also extends a welcome to every stray match end, cigarette stub and bit of paper to take refuge under it, and as it is, moreover, the favourite place for careful mothers to empty their children's sand shoes, I prefer it to stay put and try to hide some of these accumulations from view. Many times do I sweep under it and many times does it look just as untidy.

But one morning it really had been missed and that was the day when a well-known customer chose to move it to accommodate his young family in safety by a large table. I remonstrated. He was unimpressed. I brought out my reasons and excuses. He was incredulous. So much so that he suggested than when they came for coffee next morning he would expect to see me doing the front paving with the Hoover. It is impossible to win with some people. I ought by this time to be wise enough not to try!

We have strayed a little from the subject of noisy customers. There are others of these whom I prefer to call talkative, for the happy musical voices belong to parties of local ladies having an afternoon out. They come early, well before the crowds, settle themselves at the 'square' table – which incidentally is oblong – order the full afternoon tea and proceed to enjoy themselves. Everyone talks and no one listens to anyone else but it does not seem to matter.

On two occasions when we have had one of these vociferous parties, a long-suffering male happens to have been taking tea with his wife in the same room. When the time came to pay he had called me to the hall, nodded towards the happy ladies and enquired, "Have you got a parrot house in there?"

The only customers we really cross swords with are the parents of small children who come determined not to pay for them. These wonderful children, it seems, live on air, for only a small orange or milk is ordered for them – definitely nothing to eat. When the food arrives, however, excited fingers are pointed at the bread and butter or are poked into the jam. Sometimes the parents are brazen enough to say, "In a minute, darling."

So chairs are occupied, tables made sticky, floors covered with crumbs, serving plates which could be used again are smeared with jam, all, as the parents hope, for nothing. I used to try to argue with them but I now save my nervous energy and merely say, "As we charge for all children I will bring them a half portion." That settles it.

But it seems that few parents know the correct way to feed a really small child. Instead of cutting up the food into mouth-sized pieces, as was always done in our family, and popping them in neatly they allow the child to sample first one thing, then another. The result is that his plate presents a mass of bits fit only for the hen tin.

It may be mentioned here that into the hen tin goes only food that is left on plates. If I over-bake, the extra bread is given away before it becomes stale or it is eaten by the 'family' as toast. Everything else is eaten or made into puddings.

Some parents of tiny children seem quite nervous about bringing them into the café in case they should touch things. I assure them that we serve dozens of children and I long to add, "If you made less fuss they would behave quite well."

Several years ago I must have said what was in my mind to a young mother who lived for some time in the district. Recently she called again with son and daughter now grown up. She reminded me that I had said to her one day, "Expect them to behave and they will behave." I remembered that day. The children had nearly driven us wild climbing all over the furniture and giving the poor mother no peace. I had no experience of such things and was merely quoting a very successful infant school mistress whom I had known. She always said, "Parents get the behaviour they expect." I know full well that if I had been a parent my reward in that line would probably have been but small. On the other hand I should have been less than willing to live in the bear gardens that some parents we come across appear quite happily to inhabit.

If *we* feel strongly about some children, I know customers who have equally strong feelings about another matter, namely tips.

On the face of it the whole system is quite indefensible and yet, when you are on the other side of the counter you tend to view the matter differently. A special wages board for what is called 'unlicensed places of refreshment' makes recommendations about pay. They may be acceptable in some parts of the country for year-round trade. They would not attract the kind of people whom I want for helpers. Even so café wages are not high and many customers know it.

Some people, when they have been served pleasantly, enjoy giving a tip. Others want to reward the still-room worker and the washer-up who work hard but see little of the fun. They guess also that the student helpers are probably saving up for a holiday abroad. Some of them probably realise that the tips are a help to me for they keep up morale. We know it should not be so, but it is so. If the tipper gives graciously and the waitress treats tipper and non-tipper alike, little harm is done.

A waitress finds furtive tipping less than pleasant, however. If the customer can say nothing more gracious than "That's all right," she would like him to say it audibly so that she knows where she is. We do not, however, expect from everyone the Edwardian graciousness of one octogenarian customer who used to say to me, "Will you give this to the young lady who served us so charmingly." He could get away with it, many of us could not.

Occasionally elderly gentlemen mistake me for a young relative and wrap my fingers round a coin. I long to laugh for I feel once more like the little morsel with ringlets into whose palm a favourite aunt used to squeeze a sixpence. My hand knew the coin from the feel of it, for normally it was only pennies and halfpennies that found their way there, with perhaps the occasional tiny threepenny bit.

There are also the people who do not tip when they should. The ones who upset a jug of milk and have to have clean plates and saucers, or maybe they spilt boiling hot tea over the tables. The oak ones take little harm though extra polishing is necessary but such accidents usually occur on the mahogany ones and white marks are the result. For these we have to rub on an emulsion made by shaking together equal parts of spirits of camphor and camphorated oil. On such occasions we feel that a tip of some kind is called for, but it is not by any means always left.

Again there was the case of the lady who could not believe that two and nine was all that I was asking for her tea. I could have followed the example of one family-run hotel where I stayed and was charged ten per cent for service. As I did not do so I felt she might have evinced a little less surprise, letting her gratitude take tangible form instead. But enough of tips.

In such a small place my sympathy is often with the customer who easily gets lost among the many doorways and finds herself in the larder. This is probably because we store the named mugs on a high shelf in there, visible from the back of the hall.

People catch sight of them and, mentally going through their grandchildren's names, they do not realise how far they have strayed into the cake and milk department. Needless to say they are in the way there but I am not so clever at getting them out as is my present assistant. When they approach the danger zone Lilian warns them, "If you come any farther you know, you will have to work." They soon re-orientate themselves.

The wonderful standby assistant, Margaret, who was with me for about fifteen years, was Welsh-speaking though apart from some heavily accentuated syllables no one would have guessed it. Some of the Welsh customers certainly did not, for she brought us some amusing tales. One little lady said in Welsh to her companion, "Do you think we ought to leave a tip?" "No, certainly not in a place like this," was the reply.

Several of the Welsh people remarked to one another on the cleanliness of the café and they have often mentioned it to me especially in the spring after the annual stint of decorating. Keeping the house in good trim often makes people imagine that the café is newly opened and I am frequently able to administer surprises to new customers on that score. Old customers have obviously been doing tactful mental arithmetic for some years.

Because my face is round and rather juvenile and my hair not yet grey they refuse to believe how many years have rolled by. Some ten years ago a customer asked me how long I had been open. Surprised at my reply he looked at me again then remarked thoughtfully, "You must have been in short socks when you started."

People often tell me that I have not changed and are amazed by my reply, for they have not changed either though they seem unwilling to believe it. It is thirty years now since I helped at the café on Anglesey and yet people still come who say they remember me there. I can frequently administer surprises myself by calling people to mind though I am ready to admit to a poor memory for faces and an even worse one for names. But voices impress me and I remember them. Having also very acute hearing I can often go into the café prepared for the person I shall meet there. The young people do pose a problem as they change so quickly. As we are now meeting the second generation of customers it is amusing to see the children of mothers whom one first encountered in pigtails.

And how these young people have altered in style from those I met when I first started. Many years ago I was sitting in the upstairs window when a gay party of students drew level with the house. I heard one of them say, "Oh yes, it looks nice, but it would be half-a-crown a time, you bet." I ran quickly down to the door and called after them, "Oh no, it wouldn't." They came across laughing, I stated my terms and they all trooped in for a pot of tea.

I would not be inclined to do the same thing nowadays for I am getting a little tired of dim denims and dirty duffle coats. We never used to need to have the settle cushion cover cleaned twice a year as we do now.

Holiday clothes certainly tend to be old but need they be so grubby? It is strange that sartorial good manners should so often have to be brought to the attention of the young these days. Even a ladies club in London has been obliged to display notices asking that visitors should wear only conventional dress in the dining-room. A seaside café farther along the peninsula has put their request very neatly in the words,

> In your swimsuit you look fine,
> but not when you sit down to dine.

One certainly has to be prepared for all sorts and conditions of people when running a café and, on the whole, we are very lucky indeed. Many years ago I felt we had perhaps drawn an unlucky card and remarked on the rather tramp-like man I saw sitting having tea. Such exteriors were less common in those days. A very leftish friend was helping me and when I said that I hoped the customer in question would not stay long, she replied, "Why? His money is as good as anyone else's, isn't it?" I replied that it was but that other things about him might not be.

In this particular line the only people we can really complain of are the elderly ladies who are wearing their spring coats for the first time and smell strongly of camphor. We also served a family once who perfumed the whole room. They were obviously seaborne and came in battened up in navy-blue cable-stitch. Mother was not having the moths at her handiwork so had over-wintered their gear in the camphor-wood chest. On a boat in a strong wind they would hardly have been noticed but in a small café it was a different matter.

We certainly have some hilarious times in the summer at the expense of some of our more extravagantly garbed customers. No afternoon, however, produced a better crop of specimens than an August one last year. Outside on the left I was in charge of a stone-age family of nine. Or was it two families for there were four small boys of much the same age? All had gilded accents. The Welsh student was coping on the other side with a grizzly bear and his two equally swarthy and hirsute companions. Anyone passing that afternoon could have been forgiven for thinking he had stepped back into the Middle Ages. Indeed Chaucer's pilgrims must have appeared *soignés* compared with the *'tableau vivant'* to which my elegant little house was called on to provide a backdrop that day.

Perhaps we did occasionally number the famous amongst our customers but if so they passed undetected, for which they were no doubt grateful. A very well-known actress, however, who used to have a house nearby, was unable to escape into anonymity. Her deep-toned voice announced her presence as unmistakably across our little harbour as it did across the London footlights. She came in only occasionally and usually chose a quiet time for her visit. Her zest and the vibrant tones of her voice seemed to fill the house and almost overwhelm us. Kyffin Williams lived for a short time in the district after he left the army and while he was doing an art training. At his mother's suggestion he brought small limpid water-colours for me to see and asked most diffidently if I would sell them. I am sorry now that I did not buy them myself. They would be valuable now.

A few years later, the local Group, launching itself with a show of paintings in the café invited him to exhibit with them. The pictures which he brought along then were more in the style which we now associate with his name, dark and sometimes rather gloomy and powerful oils. But it was the same modest humorous artist who brought them in, quietly put them down for the Group to hang and slipped away unobserved. The only other well known artist whom I met at Borth-y-Gest was Mr Pitchforth. He loved to talk but I found that his deafness made conversation difficult. Several artists who have had their work exhibited at the Academy and the Salon live or have holiday cottages in the district. They make shows at the local galleries really interesting, besides giving inspiration to amateurs. They also show their pictures in hotels, restaurants and country houses and the visitors, no longer interested merely in prints, are buying originals. To compare the shows in the district with one that I saw a few years ago in a similar sort of locality in the south of France, Cagnes-sur-mer, the home of Renoir, is to realise how lively is provincial art in our island.

The appearances of our other 'celebrity', Sir Vivien Fuchs, are just as elusive as those of Kyffin Williams. The family used to come down with their wonderful boats. They would be out all day but always found time to take the village boys for thrilling and drenching outings in the bay.

As I am one of the cold footed ones, Polar exploration fills me with horror rather than with excitement, so I should have even less interest in it if I had not known Joyce Fuchs at university where we did practical chemistry at adjoining benches. For this reason if for no other, I listened in when she was seeing her husband off on one of his voyages. When she was asked where the family took their holidays I was amused to hear her noncommittal reply, "Oh, we just go down to an unknown little place in Wales."

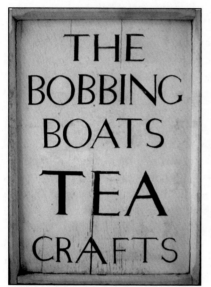

The front and back of the sign that used to hang outside the café.
It is still in the village at Richard Walwyn's house.

Chapter VII

Improvements

Desiring this man's art and that man's scope,
With what I most enjoy contented least.
From Shakespeare's *Sonnet 29*

One day in about 1948 I was having lunch with two friends who had come to the district at the end of the war. They had settled happily. On the contrary I had just realised that I was going through one of my unsettled periods. Being born under Gemini I like to have two pots boiling. If one of them goes off for a time I feel that something is wrong. However, I grew more interested in painting. I helped to start a local group in the district and at last got as far as exhibiting with them. This seemed to fill my need for the time being. However, about ten years later I found myself quoting a friend's doctor who had told her that a woman was very wise if at about the age of fifty she made some major alteration in her life. The change acted as a stimulus and did her good, both mentally and physically. In the natural course of life a woman was by this time a grandmother and could renew contact with the young. She could enjoy them without worrying about them. This gave her the tonic she needed. An unmarried woman, he averred, should make some effort on her own account, learn a musical instrument, take up new social work, start bird-watching or, failing anything more exciting, she could order a new kitchen or refurnish the sitting-room.

I decided to acquire a cottage and modernise it. My Anglesey friend coming to stay for a weekend, we looked round together. The idea was to let the cottage furnished but she plainly thought that this was madness. She pointed out that it might deteriorate considerably when it was not in use. "And think," she added, "of getting the alteration done if you were not to be on the spot all the time." I knew how right she was for I had heard many tales. One which seemed to be almost standard was of hopeful progress that might be made while you were there to see to it. As soon as you went away, however, the men would unaccountably do the same, not to be seen or heard of again for months. "And think of all the rubbish to be cleared away," Ann added, "before you could start on the garden." Perhaps that thought finally made up my mind for me.

For in the old days there was no rubbish collected in remote parts. I had heard of purchasers of old cottages in England as well as in Wales, who had found, at a tin's throw from the back door, a huge heap representing the accumulation of years of un-burnable debris.

Perhaps this is why the Welsh, when asking you if they shall dispose of a small piece of rubbish still say, "Shall I throw it?" For generations there has been no 'away' involved in the action. One threw it as far as one comfortably could and there it stayed. Another little peculiarity of their English occurs when they are putting food away at the end of the afternoon. "Shall I keep the cakes?" they will enquire, and one is tempted to tease and reply, "No, they aren't yours." But it is no use. They know that they are not speaking English, only translating Welsh, but they continue to do it.

To return to the cottage project, my friend seemed to think that if I hoped to keep my health and sanity one house was enough for me. "Think of the decorating," she said. I did and decided that what I had on my plate already in that line was sufficient to keep me going, especially as some of the rooms had not been really 'bottomed' since I came into the house.

So I bade a sad goodbye to my cottage dream and turned to the stark reality of the hall and stairs. The ceilings were cracking and needed to be lined with firm fine lincrusta. A gap was appearing between the house proper and the added bathroom. And the stairs matting, so pretty when it started life, hyacinth blue and string colour, was looking sadly faded.

The sides of the stairs had been painted cream and needed a fresh coat at least every other year. I realised too that this light paint was the cause of the matting's shabby appearance. Toned down to a medium oak colour by means of brush graining the stairs did wonders for the matting, which now looked soft-toned instead of faded. With the balusters painted ivory and the newel post scraped and polished, the stairs looked as pretty as I felt they could. Several people at various times had suggested that I should have the sides boxed in to reduce dusting. There was quite a craze for 'boxing in' at one time and I nearly fell victim to it. However, seeing how often tiny children who could not reach the rail helped themselves up the steep stairs by holding the balusters, I realised that these constituted a considerable safety precaution. So they were reprieved and now that Victoriana is back in fashion, how glad I am! My niece told me that in 'doing up' an old house they had tentatively unscrewed the 'boxing' of their staircase to reveal slender Georgian balusters beneath! People certainly treat houses in odd ways. I still dislike the newel post that terminates my stairs at top and bottom. Any demolisher with a Georgian stair rail to dispose of would be very welcome at the Bobbing Boats. But the charming little shell turn, that brings a Georgian rail to such a dainty conclusion, would probably make one dangerously narrow spot in my little lobby.

The sides of the lobby have quite recently been treated to match the stairs but not professionally. I had grown to dislike the cream paint which spent so much of its life looking shabby. Until a neighbour handed on her bright idea, I did not quite know how to make an improvement. Now it is covered with Fablon to simulate oak and very pleasant it looks. It is a simple job to do and the plastic gives adequate protection to any floor surface which does not get a great deal of wear.

From the same source has come another useful idea for inexpensive 'rehabilitation'. I have been annoyed for a year or two by cracks which developed at the top of the skirting board, where wood and wallpaper or plaster join. Probably in my house it was caused by the constantly open door but I have seen the same unsightly condition where there is central heating. Masking tape is the answer. Stuck neatly along the top of the skirting and the bottom of the wall it can be painted to match the woodwork and will last many years. Practical it may be only where wood matches wall, yet in this cottage or small villa type of house monochrome effects are essential if we want to convey a feeling of space. Once cut your wall up with patterned papers and coloured paint and the area you are mistress of is apparently diminished by a third.

Villas built on the plan of mine which have lost their original landing window, through the addition of a bathroom, are bound to be dark. A fanlight over the front door lights the hall and I soon realised that an opaque glass window in the bathroom, instead of one with glass at the top only, would give light to the landing. But the bathroom itself is not as light as I would like and I made it worse by the casing of dark hardboard by the bath. This was chosen so that a cupboard could be cut in it to house the 'Dustette' and the 'Hoover' tools. I knew that if painted white the bottom paint would soon be kicked and chipped off, because this room serves as café toilet room too. Last year I did paint it white but, over the bottom two inches, I stuck white Fablon. I now await results.

More light, however, found its way onto the landing when at last I decided to face the necessary mess and dust and have fanlights put over the bedroom doors. I had often seen this done on long corridors in hotels and the change was certainly successful. It is difficult to imagine, however, just how much dust and dirt the removal of less than a square yard of lath and plaster wall can produce. However, Mr Roberts made the mess seem even more worthwhile by giving the fanlights hinges, so that we get, not only light, but welcome fresh air upstairs. He also put a loft ladder in for me. I now have a spacious storage place above the rafters.

About this time a long look at the big tea room depressed me considerably because the ceiling of the back portion was due to be painted. It involved three times the area of painting than was really necessary because the ceiling, though quite lofty, was beamed. The outside wall suffered from chicken pox every winter, as the poor stonework contained a good deal of rubble and absorbed the water. Years ago I had, much against my will, submitted to the necessity of having the side and back walls, which are most exposed to the wind, pebble-dashed. I considered pebble-dash to be hopelessly suburban but a practical builder had convinced me that this was the only surface capable of throwing off the rain. Walls of the age of mine had no damp course. Those built with a minute slope outwards might be lucky and remain dry. The truly vertical ones or those with a barely perceptible slope inwards, acted as he said 'like sponges'.

To cure the chicken pox I decided to have my sponge walled off from the inside and Mr Roberts, always practical and frequently encouraging, told me that hardboard 'was the job' and it would last for 'years'. As it is now 'years' since it was done, I sometimes wonder what is going on behind the hardboard and if, and exactly when, nature will re-assert herself.

At the same time the ceiling was cased in and brought down a little and the landing wall was similarly lined so that the terrifying gap and the appallingly uneven plaster no longer showed. Another winter Mr Roberts tackled the kitchen, lining all the walls and shelves with white plastic hardboard. Painting is now a job of the past and all that is necessary is a good wash down with detergent every autumn.

But, best of all, we managed to have my pretty twelve-paned window dropped about five inches. At first, we did not know whether this would be possible because a large stone might have been situated just below it. I was however in luck, all the stones below the window were flat so could easily be removed. I make the back window table into my 'office desk' for many weeks in the spring. It had often annoyed me that sitting there I could not look out comfortably onto the garden. Now I can do so and this small alteration has made an amazing difference to the feel of the room.

A French window in this position would be delightful and I was sorely tempted, when the alteration was being done, to take out the entire lower wall and have a long window put in. But I thought of the possible snags, the draught in cold windy weather and the possibility that the door might swell and be out of action in the spring, which was the time that I envisaged using it.

The room now looking prettier, I began to take a fresh look at the furniture. The round table that was needed to serve a large number in the back part of the room was never really adequate and I changed it for an oblong one with a narrow central leaf so that it could be folded to a smaller size during the mornings, but when fully opened I found that it always wobbled. A practical furniture maker explained why. If the outer leaves of an oblong table are a great deal wider than the centre one stability will never be achieved. I accordingly sold this table and was lucky in finding in Beaumaris a plain oval eighteenth century mahogany one with a camel foot. Another lucky find, near Barmouth this time, was three simple country Sheraton chairs with solid seats and splat backs. Recently I saw a picture of Nelson's cabin in *HMS Victory* and was delighted to find that the chairs had been very similar to mine.

I was less pleased to find, however, when I came to examine them that the top bar of two of them had been replaced. Instead of the satin-smooth mahogany a wood had been used which feels almost like elm, slightly rough and open of grain. That, of course, accounts for my getting them at the price that I did, for every line in them betokens good design and there is some charming detail.

A replacement such as this is not a fake, however. It would have been promptly detected by anyone but me and without any knowledge at all. It is simply a perfectly honest country repair. A pity, no doubt, that it could not have been carried out in better wood, but if it had been, the chairs would not now be in my room. Moreover, the perfect back is all the smoother and more delightful to handle for being the only one.

The chairs and table marry very pleasantly with a plain oak chest of drawers and two smaller ones which were made to my own design and to the measurement of the space I had to fill. They were produced at a Red Cross centre for paraplegics at Lyme Green near Macclesfield. Altogether while I was spending the winter in Cheshire I had thirteen pieces made there, including two large and two small cupboards, a kitchen table and a blanket chest with shelves above, the chest part made to open at the front, as I had seen an antique one in a friend's house. This we call the 'Welsh dresser' and use it for display and for storage. There was also an oak tallboy for the back bedroom. All these I carried at various times inside and in the boot of an old Austin eight and later in my Mini. One piece, the tallboy, nearly failed to arrive.

I had called in Macclesfield on my way and coming out of a shop I found one of my customers, who had a holiday cottage in Wales, fingering the rope that held the piece of furniture to the car. "I don't think you will get to Borth-y-Gest with that," he said and there and then set to work to make a proper job of it.

It would have been horrible if I had left the cupboard on the road. But my loss would not have been nearly so great as that which almost befell the antique dealer who delivered my Sheraton chairs. The chairs were to replace some spindle-back ones which in any case were due to be re-seated, so it was arranged that these should be collected at the same time. The car was a large old one but, even so, it was difficult to fit the three chairs and a passenger into it. As the seat had to be tilted the shopping basket was taken out and put to stand for a minute or two on the road. The chairs at last packed in, they set off. A few minutes later a knock came at the door and I found a visitor there with a shopping basket in his hand. "It was in the road," he said, "and people were driving round it so I thought I had better bring it in here, in case you knew anything about it." The basket revealed its contents unblushingly to the world, there was a loaf, a bottle of milk, bank book and what looked to me to be well over a hundred pounds in notes. Needless to say, the owner was soon back. However, living in Wales, she was not particularly surprised to find the contents intact.

Some years before, I began to give the house its 'second innings'. Mr Roberts had given the front a face lift. It was done, in fact, as soon after the war as timber supplies could be obtained because a new Georgian style front door was to be made as well as less ugly and ponderous bay windows. Houses in the charming little Georgian town of Beaumaris had given me the idea for these. They were to be lower with a flat lead-covered top, the glass divided into twelve smaller panes at the front and eight at each side. A building in Wilmslow gave me the precise idea that I could copy on the spot. From this I worked out the dimensions I wanted and left the instructions with Mr Roberts.

The work had to be done after I left in the autumn though the house was not closed up as my two toy-maker assistants were acting as winter caretakers at that time. They had a frightening and mess-making experience one day.

The alteration to the window shapes necessitated re-plastering the whole facade. When the men had started on the job the weather was quite mild and open, but one evening it turned frosty. The plastering had been finished and they had left, when, during the evening, the whole of the plaster fell off onto the paving below. It had, of course, all to be done again. I missed the mess and was delighted with the result. The house now looked friendly instead of slightly pompous as it had done before.

But even after this great improvement the place used not to accord me a very kindly welcome when I arrived in the cold spring weather before Easter. There could be no doors to the café rooms and these were filled with chairs and tables so their coldness used to send me scuttling to the fireside in the sitting room upstairs. But I could only take refuge there in the evening, because during the day boxes had to be unpacked, often outside in an icy wind, and piles and piles of parcels had to be opened which were too heavy to carry up. One spring I remember saying to the student who had helped me at that time for several years, "Anyone can have this place for twopence-halfpenny." And at that moment I certainly meant it.

Now things are very different for we have a spacious and warm downstairs sitting-room alias the big tea room, where there is space even to open tea chests. The evening jobs of pricing jewellery, writing letters and paying bills can be done by the fire there too. It used to be very pleasant doing these jobs in the cosy room upstairs, but so often one discovered that the letter or invoice needed had been left in the tea room and a cold journey downstairs was necessary.

In planning the conversion the first necessity was to eliminate draughts. An efficient glazed sliding door saw to this and a heavy curtain at the other entrance completes the job, though besides weighting the hem of this I sometimes have to seal it to the doorway with gum tape.

A house that is left empty for the winter must not be too draughtproof or its contents will go musty. This has been the experience of cottage owners in the district and I have avoided it in an unexpected way. For the new front door being made when seasoned timber was scarce has shrunk slightly leaving a healthy draught space at the bottom. When in residence I have a heavy oak draught excluder which I simply push up against the door.

The next move was a modern fireplace. An all-tile one was out of the question, even if I had wanted one, because in the summer I need a wide shelf above for display. I therefore chose a grey tile, one inch by six which a firm in Bangor slabbed up for me and fitted with a stainless steel surround. Mr Roberts framed it with light oak and added the necessary shelf also making a solid oak curb to match.

Few customers in the summer are aware of either of these aids to comfort for the fireplace opening is filled with a grey-painted sheet of hardboard and grey shelves holding stock stand in front of the tiles. Many, however, in a windy spring are grateful for the sliding door.

Some of the extra chairs have to be lifted into the little room each autumn but this is soon done. In any case it was always wise to move the chairs from the back of the room, for one spring I returned to find their rush seats covered with mould. The other room being on an inside wall is drier.

To complete my sitting-room-cum-office I bought two most comfortable latex-foam upholstered armchairs which friends had seen in a local shop. One of these folds into its box under a bed when not in use, the other makes the double bedroom during August into a bed-sitter for the students.

For this bedroom I had been searching the shops for a pleasant-looking towel rail. The ones at my price I did not care for and the antique one that took my fancy was sixteen pounds, so I changed my plan. Instead a dimplex heater holds the towels upstairs. In the cold weather switched on at the back of the 'office' it gives us added comfort. In the bitter spring of 1966 I do not know what we should have done without it.

A splendid excuse now presented itself for visiting antique shops. I must have a table which would fold against the wall so that the two un-needed tripods could be temporarily moved out and leave my Persian rug in sole possession of the hearth.

This rug, the high spot of the room, is a beautiful dark-toned Bokhara. It is still waiting for me to repair one frayed corner but as this tucks under a cupboard I never get round to the job. Though so old it is rather modern in shape which also reduces its value a trifle and probably accounts for my securing it at my price. For instead of being rectangular it has the outline of a cooling tower. Perhaps one member of the maker's family was worried or in poor health for some time and worked the middle stretch at too high tension. The defect makes it, if anything, more lovable.

The table which I eventually found was a medium sized oval Pembroke. The dealer who sold it to me – I found it in Wales – pointed out two of its refinements. He left me to discover its snag. Yet, though I have examined several, some smaller, others of the same size,

I have found few in my price bracket that I like better and I have seen them priced up to seventy-five pounds.

The legs are square in section, but they do not narrow directly to the floor. Instead they indulge in a pleasant second thought about two inches up. Here they return momentarily to their earlier width before completing their tapering.

The other interesting feature is the drawer which has proved most useful for storing and displaying brooches and woolly animals. Its front is not merely straight, as one so often sees, instead it curves elegantly to run parallel with the edge of the table-top.

This top, I discovered later, was lightly varnished, but as the varnish was inoffensive I left it. One day I had the chance to admire a homemade table at a neighbour's house. He explained that for the top he had used a satin-finish plastic coating. It looked so good that we agreed that he should try it out on my Pembroke. An opportunity to save polishing was always welcome.

When sanded, however, the table-top revealed a patch and in the repair no attempt had been made to match the grain. It looked as though an iron had been left to burn through the surface. Nor was this an improbable accident. For in remote farmhouses the lucky dealer can often find valuable antiques, their quality completely unrecognised, put to work in a back kitchen.

I am, however, completely satisfied with the result of the highly unorthodox treatment which has been given to my table, as the plastic coating has entirely masked the patch and I have at least one table less to polish. Moreover, I realise that I paid just about the right price for it. In the world of antiques, as in every other realm, at least in this day and age, you get nothing for nothing. The lovely mule chest in the upstairs sitting-room which cost four pounds and had a round mahogany mirror thrown in as a makeweight was bought in the thirties as was the oak bow-fronted corner cupboard for which I paid three pounds – I have recently seen its twin, but needing a good deal of feeding and polish, priced at £27.l0.0! Those days have gone for ever. Even so, if you are not too 'choosy' and know where to look, good value can still be found and so can a great deal of fun.

Now I no longer dread the cold days and dark evenings of spring and autumn. The room warmed by a bright fire and with original paintings and drawings on the wall; my own ones, gifts from a painting friend and two that I have bought at exhibitions, the room looks gracious and friendly even though its fate is always to serve as workshop first. But there is space also for tea parties and for evening film shows, without having to carry all the coffee and sandwiches upstairs.

The walls of the front part of the room were made worthy of their pictures only fairly recently. There are so many jobs clamouring for their turn in autumn and spring that year after year this part was neglected. The probable reason was the appallingly uneven plastering on the two outside walls. Different crafts are done well in different districts. Ask a Welshman to build you a stone fireplace and you will have something that will give you real pleasure for years. Give him, however, a plastering job and you will feel you could have done as well yourself.

However, a friend who had converted a house in the Ffestiniog valley told me of the marvellous qualities of 'ingrain' paper. This is made from two lining papers stuck together after one of them has been liberally sprinkled with sawdust. Pasted onto a badly plastered wall unevennesses are ironed out in a truly amazing way. Even warts are made to look innocuous. Over the mantelpiece, however, my wall displayed not a mere wart but a positive carbuncle.

It was one mid-winter that I decided to make an end once and for all to its insolence. I had been called again to the jury, so on New Year's Eve brought my nephew down with me. After sitting in court for two days we were told to appear again on the Monday. "Saturday and Sunday," I thought, "just time for the job!" So I started.

When the pictures were taken down, the ceiling, frieze and walls exhibited the colours of every kind of edible fat from the cool off-white of lard, through that pinkish margarine colour that used to go by the name of 'blush ivory' to the expensive yellow of best Welsh butter. Of these the ceiling was the darkest, but luckily Richard, then a mere six foot two, would be there to help with that.

First I tackled the carbuncle which was about the size of a restaurant dinner plate. Carefully removing the paper I was insufficiently adept to catch several loose knobs of plaster which joyfully regained their freedom. The rest of the lump was accounted for by a wedge of wood which seemed to form part of the mixed matrix of the wall, and a very narrow end of pipe. I have heard so many stories of people knocking nails into gas pipes that I did not even examine this one. Perhaps it had led to one of those charming little wall gas lamps with pink glass shades, that front parlours revelled in at the turn of the century. I just did not know, but gave the piece of wood a hard whack with the hammer and quickly prepared to cover the whole thing up again.

Now, the walls done with grey emulsion paint over the clever masking paper, and the ceiling frieze and woodwork painted white, I no longer notice the carbuncle, but revel in one of the best backgrounds for flowers that has surely ever been evolved.

I am very fond of grey and white for house painting and slightly intolerant of other colours. A coloured door, perhaps, but little else gains my approval. Grey can, of course, wander up into blue or down into green as it does so beautifully on an old house in Maentwrog and still remain a lovely foil for stone and stucco. And I always welcome the softening of white into ivory. In fact I tend to mistrust the new fadeless whites that the decorator offers. Seeing, during the last few years, the lovely stone villages of Yorkshire, with white paint nearly everywhere has confirmed me in what is possibly little other than a prejudice.

When I was in France about twelve years ago a good deal of colour was still being splashed on houses in this country. They said that no one in France apart from in the Midi could afford paint and the general impression was certainly one of shabbiness in the places I visited. Perhaps that was why a little house in Fontainebleau caught my eye. It had, needless to say, a wrought iron balcony made to look like white lace against the grey of the house and all the paint except the matching front door was white. I decided that mine should be the same. The wrought iron chairs which I had designed and had had made locally would take the place, in my case, of the balcony pattern.

I find the grey walls reduce glare in the summer and for this reason I also paint the table tops some shade of grey. Of this the oddments of paint which I can scrape together at the time really decide the exact shade.

A pink Madame Butterfly climbing rose looks truly Chinese against the soft, but not too pale, grey of the wall, and by the opposite window I have a fairly tall-growing white floribunda. But the 'front garden', to produce which beds were made against the walls when it was re-paved, rarely pleases me. It never presents the blaze of colour that other front gardens in the village achieve. A good pink hydrangea flourishes by the sign support and I hope some day to coax a small-flowered clematis along the low side wall. It is still alive after a year but I fear the slugs. One spring I had a glorious show of large-flowered ranunculus like those – but not so fine – that I had seen in Greece in April. Following a nurseryman's advice I planted slug pellets with them, as any I had put in before had failed to send up even a leaf. I shall try them in pots some day, sunk in the ground for coolness.

The other bed has chiefly grey-leaved subjects, *senecio* and a very pale form of *potentilla fruticosa*. Mixed in with these are two blue-flowered shrubs for summer, *ceratostigma willmottianum* and *caryopteris*. Neither does brilliantly, but the lovely *penstemon schönholzeri* makes up for them. Dahlias whose tubers must be by now nearly embedded in the foundations light up the two beds that hold the roses. And by the door a stoneware trough houses two geraniums which last year gave me over thirty blooms.

The door, too, is prettier than it was. The improvement to it was suggested by a neighbour who owns a cottage nearby. Being a connoisseur of all things Georgian he was kind enough to admire my new bay windows but suggested that the deeply-recessed tall narrow door looked a little mean between them. He suggested an overdoor of some kind.

Though I had admired countless Georgian houses I had never really noticed the sort thing he was meaning though I was familiar with the shell that surmounts a Queen Anne door. So I began to look round. Those in our little town could only make the door look taller. I needed pilasters at the side with a triangular pediment over. The museum in

York, where I went on a visit, provided one where I could stand in peace and make a drawing. It turned out that Mr Roberts still had some grooved chisels which had been in his family for years, so between us we decided on the details.

It is not entirely correct, I know, but being a frank reproduction I think a slight inaccuracy is more acceptable than a perfect copy. It certainly does what my neighbour said it would and gives dignity and importance to the door. I would now like to add a patterned fanlight, the design outlined by a slender tracery of wood. Instead I have considered a wrought-iron fret, moveable for easy cleaning of the glass. But this is the sort of 'reproduction' which does not please me quite enough. After a holiday on Malta, however, I have begun to think differently about the matter.

Houses in Malta are stone-built, but their plainness is relieved, not only by string courses and often a dignified cornice, but by imaginative use of wrought iron. The most severe house in a town street will have an oblong or semi-circular fanlight and cover. For there, this feature, so necessary to light the hall, is thought of in two parts, window and decorative screen. A chronic shortage of wood in the island having determined the choice of materials, the highly malleable iron has led the Maltese craftsman to a more flamboyant form of decoration than the wood-framed tradition of this country could permit. So if the window is to be cleaned it must be separate and must open from the inside. This it frequently does.

On studying the Maltese fanlights I had to admit that my objection to much of the ironwork that I had seen recently in this country was on two grounds, one reputable, the other less so. For many of these 'frets' are to my mind too simple and too fragile. Wrought iron may often appear delicate but it should at the same time be skilful and look sturdy.

So far so good, the criticism is, I think, justified. But the second objection was on the grounds of association only, for the decorations in question were often to be seen on modern houses of a type which on the whole I do not admire.

When I saw wrought iron well used, as I thought, on houses of traditional style I changed my attitude considerably. And I decided to take to the local foundry the drawing that I had made of a fanlight in St Paul's Bay.

In my case, as the fan light does not open, the wrought iron screen, and it is quite frankly a screen, has been slotted into the inside frame of the window. Held in place by joiner's buttons it is easy to remove for cleaning. In planning this little improvement, I was interested to find out that my original Malta drawing had to be considerably simplified when I drew it out to scale. Four squiggles were eliminated before I felt happy with it. As it stood it would have been far too fussy for an English house where slight severity is relieved by a tiny garden.

November Bunch – a painting by Mary Howe

Chapter VIII

The Garden

This season's daffodil,
She never hears,
What change, what chance, what chill
Cut down last year's;
But with bold countenance
And knowledge small,
Esteems her seven days' continuance
To be perpetual.

From Rudyard Kipling's poem *Cities and Thrones and Powers*

My garden is walled, which fact constitutes probably part of its charm. But not till I had been in the house some years did I penetrate to the far end through a thicket of wild raspberries. Then I realised that I was the possessor of a small rectangle about forty feet by twenty five. At the bottom there was an apple tree and the tiny building we call *ty bach* (little house), whose erstwhile use can be easily guessed. The slates, aided by a romping climbing rose 'Shot Silk', are now trying to slide off the roof so I have replaced one of them with a piece of thick glass. I now have a skylight for the mowing-machine shed which is needless to say always choc-a-bloc as only garden sheds know how to be.

When I came to examine my little paradise I found half-buried flagstones here and there which suggested that there must once have been a path round a central space, so I followed the existing 'design'. I removed the docks and other weeds from the centre, levelled it and sowed grass seed. I should first have fertilised it for the grass was soon invaded by daisies which constantly threaten to take over entirely. Selective weed killers have been tried. After their use I revel in a bright green sward for a week or so till the lawn reverts to its former depressing state.

Though the lawn does not satisfy me, it certainly pleased a small customer of three and a half one day many years ago. He had come to Borth-y-Gest as a baby and his mother had promised to bring him into the café when he was a big boy. The day came at last and they went to sit at the back window table. He looked through the window onto the garden for a few minutes, deep in thought, then turned to his mother and said, "Mummy, isn't that a lovely little lawn for Miss Howe to play on?"!

The flag slates that I found were not nearly adequate for path making, so I had to hunt everywhere for more. I am still hunting, for I have recently widened many of the paths. When I see the splendid paving that is being done where houses have been modernised I wish I had had the job done properly when the front was repaved. The difficulty is that when a man can be found to do the job I seem to be too busy to show him just what I want done. I think, however, that paths are important and I have seen charming gardens, in England as well as Wales, spoilt by poor paths and wobbly walls.

I started my paving apprenticeship young for as a schoolgirl I laid a path in our garden in Lancashire in full view of the main road. Our doctor, travelling past on the top of the tram, told my father that he had heard a workman say to his companion, "Look at 'er, takin' bread out o' men's mouths." Some wheel has certainly turned full circle since those days.

Amateur pavers in this district have nearly denuded the countryside of suitable stones. I know a bridle path with a splendid view of Snowdon. Along one side there used to be a low wall, surmounted by wire. Apart from a few loose piles of stones, useless for farmer or gardeners, the wall has disappeared and fresh wire has had to be put up. I once told a customer that I was doing some paving and had been able to bring some good stones back in the boot of the car the evening before. "Where from?" she said. "Do tell me. I've had all there are in Merionethshire."

Stones were not only needed for the paths. I wanted to have raised borders too, so that alpines could grow over the edges. I once found a wonderful collection of these on a forest road and brought some home only to find that the beach opposite the house yielded just as good ones.

I have had a great deal of fun furnishing these edging walls. Being a keen reader of catalogues I realise more, I think, than some, even including the 'Sunday Sages', what enormous choice there is. But I have, alas, lost very many promising plants, probably because I took too late, the oft-repeated advice of the alpinist, to cover my plants with shingle.

After two attempts I am still hoping by this trick to establish that gift for the flower arranger, *Oenothera riparia*. Its flowers are clear yellow, its slightly pendulous stems are soft red. In a wine glass it is delightful. In my garden, failing a good stone to hang over, (my best one is occupied by a lithospermum) it is a trifle difficult to place. For one has to find an early-flowering subject which does not mind being lightly shaded in summer by the evening primrose's trailing stems. That is if you, like me, try to cover every square foot of your space. A not too choice aubretia would meet the need, perhaps.

I have to ration myself when choosing spring subjects and entirely eschew the earliest of all; so I keep to the mossy saxifrages. I like best the smaller of these such as 'Peter Pan' and 'Pixie' and I still hope to succeed with the pale yellow 'Flowers of Sulphur'. Though most of us disdain 'London Pride' yet its tiny counterpart *Saxifraga primuloides* 'Elliott's Variety' makes a delightful cloud of clear fresh pink when the rock garden's first spring flush is fading. It will thrive almost anywhere. A trifle more slow to establish is another lover of a cool spot. Usually hidden away in the 'miscellaneous' section, it is *Saxifraga primuloize*. With flowers between apricot and chestnut red it is definitely modest but has value if rightly placed, preferably I think near brownish leaves.

I was surprised when I grew *Achillea tomentosa* 'King Edward' in the front garden to find that many gardeners had not met it. Given firm soil and much sun, it will repay you with sulphur-yellow flower heads in generous succession. Its leaves are grey and pretty. A lovely edging plant with finely cut grey leaves which up to this year has not yielded me its yellow flowers is *Anthemis Rudolphiana*. I use as a spring bedding plant what I take to be another *Anthemis cupaniana* but this is a much more sturdy, not to say rampant, subject, but still a lovely thing. Its daisies are a soft grey white. Or is this perhaps *Chrysanthemum hosmariense*? No one has ever been able to name it for me. It came to me many years ago in a bunch of Michaelmas Daisies brought by a neighbour. I put it rootless into the ground and have since populated several Cheshire gardens as well as Caernarvonshire ones with it. In addition I have sold many plants of it in aid of Lifeboat funds. *Chrysanthemum haradjanii* is another which has worked hard to keep the Lifeboats afloat; it is a foliage plant only, with grey leaves rather resembling feathers. An even more dainty subject, again with finely-cut grey leaves, is *Erodium chrysanthum*, with flowers of the same soft colour as the *achillea* but shaped like a geranium, whose cousin it is.

With these bewildering geranium relatives one must go warily for *Geranium pylzowianum*. It will infiltrate insidiously while *G. sanguineum* var. *lancastriense* (wild in parts of the north) is always ready to take over with assurance. But a nursery at Aviemore has a dwarf and less greedy form of this with a smaller flower of darker pink. And if you are clever you may succeed with the choice *G. farreri* and even be able to place the rather strident *G. subcaulescens*. If so, it is well worth the effort, for the black-centred flowers are lovely.

When in a mood to play for safety I tend to turn to the campanula family, but this is probably a mistake, for there are, as I have found to my cost, many subjects here that are quite particular in their requirements.

Apart from the kinds with slightly arching growth mentioned elsewhere – and I here repeat my dislike for the colour of the one variously described as Birch Hybrid, *C. muralis* and *C. portenschlagiana*, I am willing to try all the rest, though many have tried me sorely. *C.* 'John Innes' I find dignified and beautiful, and *C.xpulloides* var, 'G.F.Wilson', slightly disappointing. Its erect purple bells were not with me long, though certainly a little longer than the lovely offerings of *C. carpatica* var. *turbinata*, but of that anon.

A gift from a customer whose lovely garden I often visit is happily colonising the many spots where the pure colour of *viola* 'Pickering blue' is so welcome. This campanula used to be designated *C. pusilla* and is like a tiny harebell. It is now, however, frequently listed as *C. cochlearifolia*.

Though to some fanciful botanists the leaves may be like a snail, what matters far more to me is that the snail does not appear to like them. The same cannot be said of some other campanulas.

I well remember one summer morning when we all decided to breakfast in the garden, I basking happily in the compliments of the household. Near the edge of the north border a clumpy plant of *Campanula turbinata* was lifting up its luminous mauve saucers to the sun. They covered the plant completely; I was very pleased. Next day nothing was left of it; the slugs had found it overnight.

I feel rather strongly that a garden is a place for living and not merely for working, planning and looking. In fact some planning can be done from a chair while eating a hasty breakfast or a leisurely tea. The fact of living alone in the early summer, no doubt, makes this garden eating easier as quite a complicated meal can be served as 'something on a tray'.

I am not always alone, however, for a robin usually comes to see me hoping still to secure a beakful of my butter. Perhaps the colour attracts him, for crumbs placed for him tend to be scorned while he will flutter quite near and even make aerial essays at the dish. One day he found himself perched on my dark green tea cosy. Then, full of coy surprise, he flew off to hop along his favourite tunnel, a conveniently protected bird walk which the arching rose branches make of the flat topped wall.

He thoroughly approves of the low retaining walls which edge the flower borders, hopping along the paths he can find there, a plentiful supply of robin delicacies conveniently placed for him at beak height.

As far as looking is concerned, garden meals have certainly helped to cure me of a bad habit with which I hope I am not the only gardener to be afflicted. This takes the form of an anxious peering for bulbs just unfolding when all the time one could be revelling in the glories that are fully out.

Perhaps, too, my garden breakfasts have rescued some common plants from extermination as being considered unfit for the company of more splendid and pernickety subjects such as New Century lilies and the roses Joybells and Josephine Bruce. For, looking into the dark shade from my sunny pavement I can appreciate the quality of the Welsh Poppies so crisp fragile and brilliant against a background of dark green and the common yellow musk rose growing tall against the grey wall of shade.

Against the grey wall too, as well as at the apple tree's base, the over rampant *Campanula poscharskyana* comes into its own. While one catalogue describes it as 'excellent on a wall' it does not add that it is willing to climb as mine is, preferably into the shade, or anywhere that is sheltered. A glorious collection that seemed to be clinging to the west facing wall of the house looked beautiful. But wind and rain soon dislodged them leaving only the soggy muddled mass that they tend to present when grown on the flat.

The Welsh poppy that has established itself with me is a *Meconopsis* not a *Papaver*. There is also the orange of *Meconopsis cambrica*, a fine 'burnt' colour. A garden near here has a colony beside an old brick-built potting shed. Careful roguing has eliminated the yellows and now the plants are establishing themselves up the wall.

This example of the right plant, albeit a humble one, in the right place is only equalled in my experience by the colony of palest pink *Erigeron mucronatus* [*karvinskianus*] on the rocky wall by Powys Castle.

Another common plant which I tolerate in small quantities for a particular job is *Viola cornuta*. It is of delicate build and there is something a little gaunt in the way the toothed yellow or mauve flowers are presented which gives it a character quite different from the more clumpy hybrids. It is also prepared to climb and as a framework I give it the spent stems of a slender Iris known as *Iris chrysographes* 'Mandarin Purple'. Though I cut off many of the leaves and shorten others the iris still consents to give me its slightly sad flowers every June and for the rest of the summer the viola fills, though only sparsely, the untidy green gap of the iris leaves.

Most of us have a pet extravagance. It must, by now, be fairly obvious that plants are mine. Looking back over the years, however, perhaps with this account in mind, I realise that I still have in the garden the glorious red *astilbe Fanal* which I bought with birthday money as soon as my wilderness began to take shape. I have given away and sold for Lifeboat funds very many plants from it. It cost me ninepence when I bought it.

At the same time I risked another ninepence on the low-growing soft reddish orange *geum Borisii*. Alas, it faded and died for the soil was too poor. This year I decided to try again, now planted in what the Victorians would have called good rich 'mould'. Now I can enjoy the vermillion flowers which in those early days of inexperience were denied me. Difficult to place, this *Geum* is at its best, I think, with a background of purple-brown Rhus.

At the risk of boring the non-gardener with yet another name I would mention one more of my plant experiments which, lost in the hot summer of 1959, I have recently replanted. It is *Trollius ledebourii,* an orange yellow wide-open globe flower for good cool soil. Its fine colour and conspicuous orange anthers mark it out as an individual of character, and it lasts longer in water than its round-headed relatives.

Designers insist that variety of level is important when designing a garden. The framework of the two mounds which achieve this variety for me were the result of burying the decorative cast-iron railings which originally surmounted the front garden wall. When the officials came round to collect all such features mine had already been, as far as I could manage it, covered with earth, so I had to pretend that this was the only house in the terrace which had escaped that form of embellishment. I had put them in two neat piles at the bottom of the garden after they had been sawn off. One reason was that in those pre-war days it was almost impossible to get anything of that kind collected, but I felt all the time, that properly covered with soil they could prove an asset.

One mound now grows dwarf pink azaleas and the lovely white azalea Palestrina, the shrub rose Penelope, two white heaths and the slightly strident but very welcome *Oxalis floribunda*. The other mound which receives more sunshine has proved to be the only place where

Nepeta will thrive. It also makes a home for the dwarf *Plumbago* and for sunroses.

I find that dahlias winter well under the *Nepeta* growth. They invariably rot if I try the recommended treatments on them. For my garden is sheltered. As I work there in stormy weather I can hear the wind from the open sea, a mile or so to the west, as it opens its throat over the wood that crowns the hill behind. But in the garden all is peace. Tulip heads do not blow about as they do in friends' gardens in the winds of May. Even so the only really giant spike of delphiniums I have ever achieved was snapped by heavy rain in July and had to be supported by a splint. Delphiniums do not much care for lime so it must not be required to strengthen their stems. Did this happen perhaps because my soil is deficient in silicon – also a strengthener? Certainly it produces great quantities of wild goose-grass which is an indication of silicon shortage. Indeed so is any plant with hairs pointing backward from the growth tip. Wild barley is one of these and grows on any piece of spare ground it can find, and so is mare's tail.

I once saw a fine holly hedge with a huge colony of mare's tail growing under it. Did the mare's tail grow there because the holly, with its sturdy spiky leaves, had taken all the silicon from the soil? Or was it there because it could fix silicon from the environment into its structure from which, when it rotted, the holly could feed? It depends what sort of horticultural theory you subscribe to. I lean towards the Rudolf Steiner School. For, according to his teaching, a certain plant inhabits an incompletely fertile soil, not because it can do without some particular mineral. We find it there because it has the power to collect just that ingredient from the rain water and fix it in its plant body. This accounts for the fact that a poor patch of earth has been seen to produce, year after year, a slightly different crop of weeds until grass, the sign of high fertility, has finally taken over.

It is strange that our soil should be deficient in silicon for there are granite quarries in the district. I once read that granite dust was a good source of quartz, so one day I presented myself at the quarry with several boxes and a trowel. I think to get rid of me, they provided a sack, shovelled the dust in and charged me sixpence. The problem was to deal with the heavy sack when I got home. Fortunately a customer, also a keen gardener, was having coffee when I arrived and helped me with it. He seemed to think me decidedly less crazy than the men at the quarry had done.

One reason why *nepeta* is not hardy at ground level in my garden is that it is a slight frost pocket. Though the climate is mild, we get occasional frost, and when an icy airstream slides down the hill and meets the resistance of the house it settles and causes a good deal of damage. The front of the house faces southeast and most things seem safe there.

But the chief problem in the back garden is that the horizon is in the wrong place. When I visited the nursery at Codsall and saw in every direction, miles and miles of sky, I realised the situation that I am faced with. For on all sides there are buildings, hillsides and tall trees, even if they do not crowd in on the garden. So, apart from one side, and that luckily faces towards the south, light comes in only from above. The effect of this is seen when I try to grow *Eschscholtzias*, those lovers of light and wide spaces. They flower a little but they make too much leaf and grow long and leggy in their search for light.

It is strange how after reading about something you begin to notice what should have been self-evident before. For I now realise that the most bouncing paeonies I have seen in local gardens have been planted well up in the corner of a wall. There they can feed on the mortar. The same thing applies to another favourite if its needs are met in this way, laurestinus.

The distinction between 'sun' and 'shade' is something gardening books tell us little about. One is told that many subjects like light shade. Should we choose for them the spring dappling that a birch tree affords, turning to quite dense shade in the summer? Or is an open spot in a north border indicated? Here, in cold shade for the six months of winter, the plant may well be basking in sun for the rest of the year. Conditions in the wild are often a guide. I would like to grow blue anemones under my apple tree to emulate the lovely wild ones in the nearby woods. But I am told that they like lime, while I need acid conditions for my small collection of azaleas.

Imitating the conditions that one decides are necessary for certain plants can be most interesting. At first I did not trouble to do this but simply let the garden be a romping ground for subjects which grew easily. Hardy crimson and blue geraniums were my standby then, but in my friable soil most of them proved much too rampant. With, however, a selection of campanulas, early Michaelmas-daisies and sidalcias and the hectic *lychnis viscaria splendens* with palest pink geraniums and dark thrift as an edging I achieved a good splash of colour. A customer remarking that my garden was a colour scheme, however, brought me up sharp. She was certainly right but the colours I seemed to have collected, provided by a good many flowers in magenta pink, were far from being my favourites. So I set to work to remedy this defect.

I decided to introduce more spring subjects. But if I had a spring garden I was determined that it should not be the purple and yellow variety that one so often sees dominated and overpowered by aubretia and alyssum.

A depressing childhood experience had pre-disposed me to a dislike of this colour combination ever since it was suggested to me for embroidering an apron. No doubt the mistress in those economical fee-paying days (the same one it was who occasionally told us that our drawings were 'coming') had skeins of these two colours to use up.

When, from an equally economical household, I had to beg material for this venture, my mother found that she also had something to use up. I was sent to school with a sorry piece of grey cotton bearing every half inch a narrow black stripe. In these days bold appliqué with perhaps red and black cross-stitch would make such a piece of stuff fairly presentable. In those days, purple and yellow feather stitching turned out a creation which I deemed fit only for the nearest dust-bin.

As well as the usual bulbs and wallflowers, I have some aubrietias, of course, which I grew from seed. Of these I try to encourage the close-growing pure mauves as well as the pinks and wine shades. For a taller companion I like their relative the double mayflower or cardamine, while for contrast and for their usefulness in small posies, I cherish a collection of Dresden china button daisies or *Bellis perennis*, now in their fourth year. Originally obtained from seed, they are divided and fed copiously in early summer after their flowering and they have as yet shown no signs of reverting.

The nasturtium I grow is called Primrose Gem, actually a Chinese yellow, a colour relatively rare in the garden. Being something of an aristocrat it does not germinate freely. In fact, to make sure, I always sow some in pots for I could not consider a summer without them. The cherry red version is lovely too but this colour is not as rare in the garden as is the soft yellow.

One spring when they had germinated particularly badly I had the misfortune to break one off. Hopefully I stuck the broken piece back into the soil. It grew away splendidly. Since then I have read that the nasturtium is a half-hardy perennial. So I now winter a few 'cuttings' in pots in the house.

Small fibre pots are useful for raising seeds as the whole pot can be planted. Arranged in rows on a seed tray they can be quickly watered. With me, however, they have only had the success that is claimed for them, when their contents have been strong-rooted subjects. Though lavatera worked well treated so, nemophila and viscaria, to use the gardeners' descriptive jargon, never 'got away'. Their delicate roots remained imprisoned by the pot wall.

It seems foolish to suggest sowing these hardy plants indoors but the reasons are twofold; our spring droughts and our voracious slugs. And it may not be so foolish, either, because other districts, other techniques! Nursery gardeners, for example, laboriously raise boxes of white alyssum for sale. Both white and purple kinds seem almost indigenous with me and come up self-sown every year.

There is, I am told, somewhere down the middle of England a mysterious line east of which slugs are visitors but not serious pests. We are very well to the west of it.

The only protection I have devised apart from an expensive diet of poison, is aluminium lawn edging. One could make one's own with the rings from old loose-bottomed cake tins. I saw such rings used first to protect delphiniums in a friend's garden. I leave the barbican sticking up several inches round plants such as lupins and Jacob's ladders, both of which slugs love. Then when I leave in the autumn I pour generous doses of ash from the fire both inside and over the surrounding moat.

In spite of all precautions, however, the slugs are always with us, and one summer they were joined by moles. To them I owe a great debt. When I first discovered them, they were ravishing the garden turning up the shallow-rooted perennials which lay on the surface to die. I tried to smoke them out with special fumigants, but the fumes could be seen escaping through the interstices of the loose soil. I next bought poison which had to be mixed with chopped worms, and for some reason, the millions of these seething on the compost heap were deemed to be the wrong species, or was it variety? So I had to dig for them and worms inhabit the very deepest strata of our dry soil. I was a little more successful with a trap and actually caught one mole.

Thinking I should have to settle down to some sort of co-existence with my new pest it occurred to me that their burrowing noses might be discouraged if I stocked the garden with subjects having roots both strong and long. So I determined to grow roses.

I had shied away from growing them up to this time because I had seen few in the district except Albertine and another for which I accidentally found the name by buying its repeat-flowering sport, The New Dawn. My poor soil might support Albertine and Dr Van Fleet, as it was already supporting a sixpenny store version of Gloire de Dijon on the larder wall, but I could not imagine any others flourishing.

However, Margaret organised matters so that I was able to go to the Royal Welsh Show at Bangor. There I fell in love with the polyantha roses and brought copious notes home.

That winter also brought copious rain and, the headquarters of the moles being in a low-lying corner of the field behind the house, I think many were drowned in their burrows. We certainly seemed to see the end of the menace next spring.

I had to buy bags of loam to plant with the roses but I was not pleased with its quality, though it was very expensive, so I began to collect it from anywhere, short of farmers' fields, where I could find it. The edges of new trunk roads revealed several heaps where the making of neat verges had presumably proved too costly. Much of it was black and peaty but, I think, for roses, which prefer an acid medium, probably none the worse.

In the bed surrounding the apple tree I planted hybrid teas and polyanthas. The site is not perfect for them and I ought to take out Josephine Bruce and replace her with an easier-going polyantha rose. But Rosemary Rose does splendidly and I can cut armfuls of her flowers from one bush. Liking to try as many varieties as possible, I have made this into a bed of mixed reds and I like the effect. It is fun after admiring what the rosarians call the classic pointed buds of Mme Louis Laperriére, to enjoy the crimpy pompoms of Garnetté, after the elegant rosette shape of Red Favourite to be reminded of the old roses by the velvety quartered blooms of Geranium Red. I like the colour effect too, especially as seen from the house.

As excuse for this little experiment I have good authority in Lawrence's picture 'The Red Boy'. I once read that the velvet of Master Lambton's suit is made up of several different colours, scarlet, cherry, vermilion, crimson, hence the glow and life of the fabric. My mixture of dark De Ruiter's Herald and glowing Moulin Rouge, is lighted up by the gay clear red of Hobby, Border King – a small single flower but a lovely raspberry red – and the dwarf Meteor which clashes gloriously with them all. They used to be overtopped by Frensham but I did not care for its flowers so I am trying Fervid instead.

Roll on the day when nurseries will employ women to describe their roses. As things are, no better adjective than 'orange scarlet' can be found for the lovely soft red of the pillar rose 'Danse du Feu'. Visiting, one day, a friend whose colour tastes are similar to my own, I found on her wall the red rose I was seeking. The colour of it reminds me of a piece of silk which I cherished as a child. I was an inveterate dresser of dolls, but this piece of soft red silk was never cut up. It stayed instead in my bit box. It might, perhaps, occasionally be draped round Freda of the black eyes, but it was always put back intact. I have *Danse du Feu* now and can gaze at it to me heart's content.

Years ago I used to read Gertrude Jekyll. She was a true artist in that she believed the end to be more important than the means. With her, it did not matter how you achieved your results provided you were successful. And though herbaceous borders are no longer feasible in many gardens, her way of achieving success with them can be followed just as well in the shrub borders of today. She was not above 'dropping in' spare plants in pots if an unlovely space yawned. My treatment of geraniums and especially of begonias enables me to follow her advice as well as giving the plants the tight root conditions they prefer.

Would that some-brave soul would experiment with roses! Would it not be possible to move them in October? Why should the nurserymen be so determined that no bundle of roses shall pass through their gates before November the first? It seems the idea is that on this date they all become dormant. But this is not so for they often go on flowering almost till Christmas. Yet how many of us receive, not our order, but a note from the nursery regretting that the weather is 'unsuitable for lifting'. When we finally receive the roses, what has happened to the weather in our garden? It is, of course, 'unsuitable for planting'. The nurserymen could well make life easier both for us and for themselves by adding the second fortnight of October to their 'lifting season'.

But let us return to our other prophet Miss Jekyll. She did not depend on potted plants only for her 'dropping-in' tricks. She found that the herbaceous campanulas would move even when in flower. Following her advice, I let the persicifolia types follow my honesty plants which are so useful to give height to the border in spring. A good watering for a day or two and the campanulas are happily established and carry on for the rest of the summer.

I have tried many spreading campanulas. Of the ones that consent to thrive I like the pale C. *garganica* 'hirsuta' best. This is a lovely pure mauve with none of the overlayimg of vague pink which the nearly-related Poscharskyanas exhibit. A delicate ice blue variety of these useful campanulas is called C. *Poscharskyana* E.K.Frost. It rather resembles the house-plant sold (erroneously) as Star of Bethlehem. I also cherish a dusty pink version. With the pink *Scilla hispanica* this is the only plant I know which contributes just this shade to the garden. Perhaps because their colour scheme contains a certain amount of brown, both these flowers are lovely with brown leaves, the early ones of astilbes or later the pewter brown ones of the despised ajuga.

Particular gardeners might not be anxious to welcome the ajugas and lamiums, alias the bugles and dead nettles which I grow in mine. However, I use them as ground cover, because they give a variety of colour which flowers cannot offer. There is, as a matter of fact, a bugle of the most deep and telling blue which is lovely next to *Alyssum* 'Dudley Nevill', a yellow ochre variant of the rather brash one so often grown. It also goes well with its cousin *Lamium maculatum* 'Aureum' which has a lime yellow leaf. A large patch of this plant lights up the shadier end of my shady border, doing the job that *Tanacetum parthenium* 'aureum' [golden feather] or pyrethrum used to do in the municipal park in my youth. But instead of marching with calceolaria and echeveria, it melts into an herbaceous most pleasantly.

Plants in the wrong place may be a definition of weeds, but it is amazing how few plants in the right place can make the nucleus of a garden. For the right place means not merely the place they grow best in. It is the one where they show best amongst the most suitable associates, where they take on an extended personality. And they convert the addict who groups them thus from mere grower into gardener. For it is our gardens which make us into gardeners. It is they that pose the problems in whose solution we learn the gardener's art.

What pleasure is given us by successful grouping. It may for much of the year be but a collection of foliage plants but for some reason they please us even though the small addition that we feel would finish the picture presents a problem. The perfect plant or shrub for colour, height or season does not thrive in the given situation. And now the hunt is on, appetite is whetted and observation of plants in our own garden, or groupings of those in other people, reveals the breadth, the demands, the possibilities of the task we have embarked on.

Often our successes occur in what are known as 'difficult' places. For these are like the backward child. We lavish on these spots attention that we deny to the easier reaches. They may even become the parts of the garden we most frequently visit. And moreover they spread over the rest of our motley plot those qualities of repose which help to knit into the artistic whole, which we every new season dream of its becoming.

My other one-tone effects seem to be in yellow. Creamy yellow broom in one forms a background for the primrose yellow *Rosa Cantabrigiensis*. This is a little like Canary Bird, but perhaps a trifle less vigorous and the prettiest leaves which turn a soft brown in September. They do double duty with the ivory collection. And easiest of all is the green stem vase filled with, not merely the flowers, but whole sprays of pale yellow nasturtiums. Leaves, twining stems and even developing seeds will, after an hour or two, orientate themselves to the light, to festoon from the vase as if they grew there. This is also the right and the best way to cut sweet peas. For their own foliage and the way they grow 'on tiptoes for a flight' reduces the slight formlessness of the flowers, which seem to be the price we have to pay for their glorious scent.

For less aristocratic subjects more dramatic treatment is needed and then it is that colour contrast can be so exciting. In one miniature that I like there is contrast of form too, for I mix round and plumpy orange marigolds with the slender grace of purple buddleia, or I vary the theme using orange Welsh poppies, almost a weed with us, and dark purple blue iris.

For it is chiefly to supply flowers for cutting as well as to give a pretty picture from the back of the tea-room that the garden exists. Though I have many favourites among flowers, yet I have to allow soil and situation and the needs of the vases rule my choice. If I had more time I might succeed with many things that I have long ago despaired of growing. On the other hand, being a compulsive gardener, limitation of time is probably salutary for me. The success I long for is out of my reach so I stop worrying about it. Instead I enjoy the garden and I enjoy, too, arranging its harvest for the house and planning what to grow with this hobby in mind.

Chapter IX

Conclusion

That is where the manuscript ends. Mary may have intended to write more but if she did so her efforts have not survived. The house still stands and looks much as it did in its heyday as a café. Internally there have been alterations aimed at making it more suitable for its present role as a holiday let. It is still owned by Mary's family and will probably continue to be so for many more years. Editor

A photograph of Mary in her tearoom showing the many items for sale there

*The fanlight designed by Mary Howe which features in the
chapter headings (Photograph by Cathy Woodhead)*

A sketch by Mary Howe with the Bobbing Boats on the left

Some of the other people who helped me about that time have told me that I was sometimes testy and hard to please. I insisted, for example, on matching up cream jugs and sugar bowls and the tiles we used for teapot stands. The tea things were the same banded design that we had started with but they were now a warm tan brown. So a variety of colours contrasted pleasantly with them, greys, brown, greens and turquoise shades. Done as I liked it done, the effect was very pleasant. Mixed up at random every piece lost its value.

I was probably unnecessarily fussy but, as some of the people were with me for several months, I thought that they could really have mastered it. If they had taken the trouble they could have worked out the problem for themselves instead of rather grudgingly trying to please me, or just hoping for the best. My occasional fussiness about what I considered to be 'artistic' details was the only cause of friction that we encountered in all those years. On the whole we seemed to fit in very happily. I was lucky to find at least six long-term helpers who were as enthusiastic about café-running as I was. They were pleased to have found a café in which to gain their experience. I was glad to have found them. In happy routine the summer sped by; they, sorry to feel their time at Borth-y-Gest passing so quickly, yet at the same time planning and looking forward to a place of their own; I, carried along as I tend to be by the day-to-day life of the place.

Time never hung heavily; there was always so much to be done. And, older now and perhaps a little more experienced, I learnt amongst other things that when tired or a little depressed, it is wise not to survey life in a general way; it will appear far too grey. It is better to fix on one cheerful facet of it, or if none seems to present itself, then force oneself to 'count one's blessings'. In the mood of the moment this will probably not take long, but the attempt seems to release a bubble of satisfaction which rises and carries one's spirits up with it.

It may be that I am, as one of my school fellows called me, 'one of the merry ones'. Perhaps it is more true to say that business has been the tonic I need to take me out of myself, by its constant and pleasant stimulus. The only time, in fact, when I used to feel flat was when the evenings drew in at the end of the season, particularly if poor weather brought a sudden lull in custom. The happy busy house would seem strangely quiet then, and something seemed to be wrong. Now a mixture of 'philosophy' and house refurbishing has made this time a good deal happier.

And there is, of course, always the garden. If as usual, it falls below one's expectations and hopes, still, as Kipling knew so well, a time spent wrestling with it if it is not behaving well enough to give us pleasure, can at least send us indoors afterwards feeling more in tune with life. But I realised too that there might be another factor to account for my occasional moodiness. I felt that the place was slipping out of gear: proportion was being lost. I had for several years enjoyed helping to train other people to run cafés. I would now for a change have the fun once more of working actively on my own.

Apart also from helping to give prospective caterers the same kind of help which I have gained in Anglesey, I have been interested to hear of at least two cafés which owed their existence in the first place to having seen mine. I went to have tea at one in Cheshire. The house had been specially built for the purpose and I was shown the beautiful kitchen and was able to admire the immaculate tiled floor. I was not, however, greatly surprised when I heard that, after a spell of years, the owners had decided to sell as they had found the standing too much for them. Probably if I were running a café all the year round my feet would have given in long ago, but I wondered how much the tiled floor had, in this case, contributed to the inevitable tiredness.

To return to my own problems, at this point I decided to try to work with a much smaller staff and the experiment was a success. A part-time helper who lived quite near gave me more of her time. She understood my ways perfectly and she helped to train the students and occasional helpers who filled in at the busy times.

Of these I seemed to find a wonderful variety. There was an air hostess who caught a very bad cold so giving me the excuse of suggesting that the climate did not suit her. For the place did not afford her the scope she needed, so she found a job in Cornwall and found a husband there too. She left her friend behind whose company I enjoyed enormously. She was not the only one who was trying her hand at writing, for another girl who helped me wrote short stories for Canadian magazines. A friend of a friend who helped me had lived *au pair* in Norway where the family went out skiing in swimming togs. After the heat of their house it was probably a form of sauna bath.